STICKY LEADERSHIP

. . . .
**HOW SUCCESSFUL
ENTREPRENEURS
GET THEIR LEADERSHIP
to STICK in the HEADS,
HEARTS and
ACTIONS of OTHERS**
. . . .

LARRY BRIGGS

eSuite Press

www.esuitepress.com

Sticky Leadership

Published by Larry Briggs

Copyright © 2015 by Larry Briggs

ISBN 978-0-9971-0460-8

CONTENTS

Acknowledgements

To Anna and Jan
I couldn't have done this without you.

. . . .

Thank you to:

This book would have never happened without the help of the amazing leaders I've worked with over the years. I've learned from you. For this I'm grateful. You have made this uphill journey rewarding.

To those close friends who first believed me when I initially talked about writing a book, but began to snicker after years of nothing happening; thanks for not giving up on me. Despite my struggles in getting it right after twenty-five years I can testify that there is power in never quitting.

The few who read my early transcripts know they were dry and philosophical. Thanks to my editor and writing coach Steve Halliday. The really good parts of this book are from you and your influence. You are a unique talent and I'm honored to work and learn from you. Your vision for convergent media is inspiring; keep sharing it till the tools show up and you change the publishing world.

And finally to all those I have had the privilege of working with intimately including the hundreds of consulting and coaching clients; John Bernard in the launch of Mass Ingenuity; John Gorman and Hap Clark and all the people I worked with in the early years of Timberline Software; and those from my youthful experiences with Institute Data and Pacific Data systems in the Guam days—this book contains what you taught me and what we learned together. Thanks.

MAKE THE DREAM HAPPEN

W hat do you want your leadership to impact right now? As a good leader, you have a big idea or vision that inspires you. It's so big, in fact, you know you can't accomplish it on your own. You know it requires a motivated team to come alongside you so that together you can make it happen. You know that great leaders attract, motivate and gather the people and resources needed to make that dream a reality.

But you also know it's easier said than done.

"Randy" started his business five years before I met him. In the beginning, he kind of liked the feeling in his gut whenever he took a risk—like blending the anticipation of a wicked rollercoaster ride with the feeling he got as a high school wide receiver when he went for a touchdown pass as the clock ticked down. In this case, he risked stepping away from his job as a wildly successful dental equipment sales rep for a large, national firm to start his own business selling replacement parts through a mail order catalog. Dentists who bought equipment from him continually complained about expensive repair and replacement parts, and his new idea seemed very sound.

Although the Internet had not yet become a reliable sales channel, Randy could easily imagine producing an attractive catalog full of repair and replacement parts and building a company to handle the orders such a catalog would generate. But he had no idea that his simple dream would evolve into a small component assembly business, requiring him to find and manage people who could effectively service his expanding customer base.

As the business grew more complex than he'd ever imagined, it also got increasingly hard to keep his customers happy. And he felt stuck. Getting people to do what he needed them to do, on time and in the way he needed it done, had turned into a nightmare. The exhilarating days of the grand adventure had vanished long ago. Today it felt more like a frustrating grind. The people skills that had worked so well for him in the sales game now seemed to fail as, once more, he had to confront an employee who had screwed up an order.

In our first meeting, we sat across from one another in a restaurant. As he got ready to speak, he gripped the table so hard his hands turned white. "If this doesn't get more fun," he said to me, fire in his eyes, "I'm out of here."

Maybe you feel stuck, like Randy, laboring to get people on board with your big idea. You had hoped to get them to do things in the way you wanted them done. Things would go much faster and better if I could just do it all myself, you've thought. It seems as though the chore of getting everyone to work together to accomplish the vision can become almost as big a task as the idea itself! And so you've wondered, When did this thing become so much about people? When did it turn into a big, complex, time-consuming, emotionally draining struggle?

Maybe you feel like that right now. If so, allow me to let you in on a little secret:

Leadership is tricky unless it is sticky.

This "sticky" kind of leadership sticks in the heads, hearts, and actions of your people. It gives them a potent desire to work with you and their colleagues to accomplish a big goal. At the best of times, it feels almost effortless. Sticky leadership has certain viral qualities that, over time, tend to migrate from you to your closest associates, and then spread from them to others. Sticky leadership avoids manipulation and empowers your people to grow and become more of who they were really meant to be. Believe me, they notice! And when they do, they will feel inspired and energized . . . and they will come to you for more of it.

It's All about Results

Regardless of how many books on leadership hit the shelves, the search continues for the Holy Grail, that glorious secret that will transform us into stellar leaders with the power to change the course of history and make our dreams come true. And so we jump from leadership book to leadership book, looking for the one that will have THE answer for us.

After spending nearly three decades focused almost exclusively on leadership, I've learned a critical lesson: It's really about results. The one undeniable product of leadership is the results it generates. Successful leadership has a profound influence on the way others actually behave and think.

One can quickly disrobe an author and his or her works by looking at the lives of those the author has trained or mentored. What impact do we see? Do we note any proof of results-producing leadership? Do these leaders actually do what they profess, and can observers detect any evidence to back up their claims?

May I suggest that the best way to measure the effectiveness of any approach is to test it? See whether its insights make a difference in your own leadership. The same thing is true here. I encourage you to test the insights and concepts in *Sticky Leadership*. Apply what you read here to your life (the workbook will really help you) and then let me know what results you get. Hold me accountable for the truths I've unpacked here!

I choose the word "truths" very carefully, because if the information in this book "works," it won't do so because it's mine, but because it's true. Truth is truth. What works has worked and will continue to work, simply because it's true. What is unique about this book is the packaging and the perspective I've provided to help the concepts come alive.

I am a great believer in simplicity on the other side of complexity—but we can't get to that simplicity without first wading through the complexity (and often the confusion). In *Sticky Leadership*, I aim to challenge your thinking, entertain you a bit, and motivate you to use the truths you find in this book to make the trip from complexity to simplicity.

You'll see that it works!

Most entrepreneurs I know are searching for sticky leadership, although they may not use that name. "But I don't consider myself an entrepreneur," you say. That's okay; read the book anyway. Nearly all the leaders I've known have a good chunk of the entrepreneurial spirit.

I know entrepreneurs, because I've served them for decades. I admire them immensely, mostly because they play with "skin in the game." True entrepreneurial leaders invest themselves fully in whatever they want to make happen, whether it be a venture for profit or non-profit. For entrepreneurs, it's all very personal . . . which makes it all very real.

Entrepreneurs have learned that they need to discover what isn't working for them and then stop doing it, lest it cost them dearly. An entrepreneur gets to live another day only if he or she can create, invest, measure, and then prune well. Cash is king in the entrepreneurial world, and these leaders invest much of their own. This investment often comes in the form of deferred wages and deferred gratification—and that makes them unique, as it runs counter to the self-gratifying, instant-reward mindset of our culture.

Sticky leadership is important to entrepreneurs because they know they always have more to do than they can get done (a difficult realization, since entrepreneurs have little trouble seeing what's possible—and it's agony for them to have to wait for it). To accomplish the desired goal, they recognize they must get others aligned with their vision. They need co-laborers who will pitch in and work with the same kind of seriousness and sense of "skin in the game" that they themselves embody.

Over the years, I have identified three crucial traits that allow sticky leaders to create this kind of "viral transfer of leadership." Each trait builds upon the previous one in a way that reinforces all of the concepts.

First, sticky leaders learn to love uphill. The daily challenge of facing yet another obstacle, recovering from a failed plan, addressing a shortage of resources, or regaining momentum after a market disappointment doesn't get them down, but serves to re-energize them for the uphill climb to fulfill the vision. There is both a psychology and a process to learning to love uphill. Once mastered, it creates a reinforcing loop that keeps sticky leaders going when others want to quit.

Second, sticky leaders lead from the inside out. It all starts with them personally. They know that if they lack authenticity in the uphill climb, others will smell their failure to be real and won't buy in. A sticky leader's "stickiness" starts with who he is as a person, in the core of his (or her) being. That kind of stickiness helps others to mirror much of what the leader does, how he or she thinks, and the way he or she spreads positive influence within the organization. But it doesn't end there! Inside out leaders tackle head on the obstacles presented by uphill challenges. The leader's ability to change what is occurring right now is key to others feeling attracted to him or her. This magnetic quality ultimately creates a leader /follower dynamic that spreads to others—the coveted viral transfer of leadership.

Finally, sticky leaders know how to create a game worth playing. You know as well as I do that having skin in the game, combined with being critically self-aware and accepting the unanticipated challenges of the uphill journey, can create a heavy and (at times) even depressing burden. Creating a game worth playing helps every leader maintain a positive perspective that can make even the most challenging times seem fun. I've not met any entrepreneurs worth their leadership salt who didn't talk about the fun of their work. Creating a game worth playing makes it possible to share the fun with others in highly productive ways, in large part by engaging others in a shared, attractive vision.

You will see how games and game theory can help bring rhythm and perspective to what, at times, can frankly feel overwhelming. The stickiness of your positive influence makes achieving the venture both possible and fun.

When you start seeing these three traits working together in your own life—Learn to Love Uphill, Lead from the Inside Out, and Create a Game worth Playing—you will begin to see real results where you most need a breakthrough.

Let Me Be Your Coach

For the last twenty-five years, my life's work has been coaching business executives. A good coach always begins with a question to learn what exactly the client wants to accomplish. One of my mentors said, "You can't tell what is going on here (pointing to his head) if you can't make noise come out of here (pointing to his mouth)."

So let me ask again: What do you want your leadership to impact right now?

A good coach engages your thinking and makes it possible to listen to yourself so you can begin to see and then understand what you hadn't previously recognized about your thoughts, feelings, and actions. Finally, the coach helps you to apply these discoveries and observations in a way that allows you to obtain whatever benefit you seek.

Would you like to learn and master the art of sticky leadership? If so, I'd be honored to serve as your coach. I've written this small book so that you can experience and reflect on sticky leadership in a way that equips you to accomplish your big dream, whatever it is. What you learn here really can make it possible for you to accomplish the things that you consider most important.

Why am I so confident I can help you to achieve all these things? For one thing, I've been a student of leaders and of leadership all my life. But a second reason is almost more important. I've become a sticky leader, even though I fall into the category of "reluctant leader."

From my earliest days, I remember my father telling me, "Larry, you are a leader and you are going to do great things in this world." He then looked toward my younger brothers and sisters and added, "All these kids are looking up to you."

As the eldest of nine siblings, I learned at an early age about responsibility. Mom leaned heavily on me to help care for my brothers and sisters, particularly during my middle school years, when it seemed as though a new baby joined us every year. I didn't particularly like or want the responsibility, but my dad's words continued to ring in my ears.

Even back then, I remember thinking, What the heck does it mean to be a leader? And if I'm supposed to be one, why do I feel like such a failure when I'm put in charge? None of these kids seems to like or respect me, even though I'm trying hard to be the leader Dad says I'm supposed to be!

You know what? The problem doesn't go away just because you become an adult.

How many times as a leader have you done your best to get something important to happen, but it seemed as though your people didn't really care or, at best, told you only what they thought you wanted to hear? They gave you lip service but acted contrary to what you knew needed to happen to accomplish the goal that would serve everyone's best interest.

Sticky Leadership addresses that problem head on.

As I introduce you to sticky leadership, you will hear more about my story and learn how I moved from being a reluctant leader to becoming a sticky leader. Today, I can enthusiastically say that I love leadership and what it does to make our world a better place. I'm glad to say I've helped many others embark on a similar journey.

Now it's your turn. Are you ready to make your dreams come true? Are you ready to bring to life your vision? What do you want your leadership to impact right now?

Part One

LEARN to LOVE UPHILL

We all know what it means to feel thwarted. Stuck. Stalled. Hung up. It can seem like a bad dream, the kind in which you're frantically trying to run away from some threat, but you just can't get your legs to move.

At times, leadership can feel just like that.

When we find ourselves in such difficult times, we need a breakthrough. We need, quite literally, to break through whatever is holding us back.

Most of my clients are entrepreneurs who have built businesses using their enormous gifting, energy, and clever thinking. I've noticed that the successful ones create going concerns with the strength to survive both unexpected downturns and demanding growth spurts. But at some point, they all find themselves stuck and needing help to get beyond some major obstacle.

Where do you need a breakthrough? Is there a place in your life or in your business where you have become stalled? Where does it feel as though you're parked alongside the freeway, not moving an inch, as others go whizzing by? Where does your work most deeply frustrate you? In such difficult spots, we all imagine the way to get back to zipping down the highway is to keep doing more of what got us here. Just work harder! we think.

But that isn't smart uphill leadership. And almost never does it work. By pushing the throttle all the way to the floor, you'll surely get the wheels spinning faster—but you'll remain stuck, burning far more energy just to go nowhere. Merely applying more of your personal gas rarely works and it isn't sustainable. You need a breakthrough and you need it now.

Sticky leaders who practice Uphill leadership know something you don't. They know how to convert obstacles into breakthroughs by changing one important thing that, over time, changes everything.

SIX STEPS to a BREAKTHROUGH

"Jim," the founder of a marketing agency, came to me with a stubborn obstacle. He really needed a breakthrough. We had met the year before during a visit to Africa. I was serving a client there and he had come as a fund raising expert to help a charitable organization. Jim has a great ability to match non-profit organizations with donors.

Back in the States, I had lunch with Jim and his wife to discuss his leadership obstacle. He confided that his thriving business had begun creating big problems for him at home and in his marriage. It's a common story: A personal or business success turns into an obstacle and a problem to be solved.

One of Jim's most successful services involves holding radio events around the country where he uses his deep experience in his field and his valuable on-air radio talents to conduct fund raising programs. His intimacy with the cause and his ability to package this information into a compelling story that resonates with listeners has helped him to build a thriving business.

The problem? Jim himself had become the constraint in his business system. As he took on more and more enthusiastic clients, his family began missing him more and more at home. A major conflict quickly mushroomed between Jim's commitment to being an involved husband and father and his commitment to his business partner, their employees, and the growing client base of worthy organizations that really did need the company's services. Jim had tried just working harder, but that solved nothing. He began traveling more often than he and his family wanted, often for back-to-back events in various cities, flying at night to reach a destination just on time and then doing his thing the next morning. It all became exhausting. Even though the success he achieved yielded multiple rewards, it had begun to take a toll on his personal wellbeing. Coming home drained to a family that greatly missed him, with the kids continually asking him, "Daddy, will you be able to come to my game on Friday?" or "Why do you have to leave again? You just got here!" wore heavily on Jim's heart.

So it didn't surprise me terribly that at our lunch a few years ago, Jim's wife looked at me across the table and pointedly asked, "Larry, can you fix this for us?"

The Kink in the Hose

It may be that, like Jim, you've become stuck because you're doing all the most important stuff yourself. You yourself have become the constraint in your business system.

Or maybe you just can't figure out how to get over some hump. Revenue remains flat despite everything you've tried.

Or perhaps the market has shifted, while you haven't, and you find yourself working ever harder just to make the same amount of revenue.

Or possibly, as with Jim, your constraint takes on a more personal nature. Your job no longer feels fun and your family life has begun to suffer because of the huge amount of time you must invest in the business.

Leaders of companies reach this frustrating stage for myriad reasons—and this is where sticky leadership can make all the difference, since sticky leadership is all about converting obstacles to breakthroughs. But how does that work, exactly? Where do you begin?

You start to turn the corner when you learn how to Love Uphill. And the first step in learning how to Love Uphill is to find the most obvious and controlling obstacle (or constraint) that you need to convert into a breakthrough.

Think back to last summer, when you watered the flowers in your yard. Although you turned on the spigot full blast and pointed the hose at the flowers, you got nothing but a weak trickle. What had happened? You're sure that you fully turned on the spigot. What should you do to fix the problem?

We all know the answer. You have a kink in your hose. The water doesn't flow as it should because, somewhere, a kink in the hose has created an obstacle.

Leadership constraints work in nearly the same way. We have an idea of what we want to make happen, we have launched our plan, we have pulled together all the necessary resources . . . but the results we want just don't show up. What's the problem?

There has to be a kink in the hose somewhere.

A breakthrough is simply removing that kink in the hose— the constraint or obstacle—so the results we expect can flow freely.

Converting an Obstacle to a Breakthrough

While getting the kinks out of the hose in your leadership challenge isn't quite as easy as in our analogy, it isn't that hard, either. All of us can tell when we're bumping up against some constraint. The kink in the hose becomes more and more obvious, as does the certainty that we need a breakthrough.

Success tends to beget obstacles; that's just the way the process normally works. One way or another, the success we achieve also creates one or more kinks in the hose. So how do we "unkink" the hose? How do we get the water flowing again? The process of converting an obstacle into a breakthrough involves six simple steps.

1. **Identify the constraint.**

   A constellation of issues can create multiple kinks in the hose, so look for the dominant constraint. Look for the one that, once relieved, will take with it all (or at least most) of the other, smaller kinks. Be careful not to land on the first obstacle that just happens to come to the surface! Look for the controlling constraint that impacts all the rest.

   In Jim's story, the dominant constraint in the system was Jim himself. The company had only one person, Jim, who could do the on-air talent job of telling stories and encouraging donors to give.

2. **Get intimate with the current reality.**

   Once you find your kink in the hose, embrace it. Get extremely familiar with it. Take the time to understand what it is and why it is happening. Closely examine the problem, who is involved, how it came to be, and the impact it is having on the rest of the system. What do you and others think about this constraint?

   I sometimes find that the language we use to describe our constraints can become self-limiting. I often hear language like this:

   "We just can't..."

   "It's always..."

   "They just never..."

   "There is no one around who could ever do as good a job as..."

   "There is no way that we could ever..."

   We invite these sacred cows to surround the constraint, which only makes it harder to remove. It'd be like saying, "Yes, I know the kink in the hose is preventing me from watering my flowers, but it's such a pretty kink! Just look at its beautiful curves. I can't bear to think what the hose would look like without it." Who would ever say such a thing?

As we learn to Love Uphill, we have to completely embrace the truth of the current reality and not gloss over the evidence (however uncomfortable), how people feel or think about it (however unpleasant), and the apparent difficulty in eliminating it (however challenging). We need to address all of it, in its entirety.

At times, this may seem to cause the constraint to grow larger and more difficult. But this isn't a bad thing! We want to intentionally make it BIG so that everyone can see it for what it really is.

Every constraint has elements we would classify as both good and bad. In the process of embracing the constraint, however, never overemphasize either the good or the bad. Those are just relative terms that tend to polarize us and even prompt us to reject important elements of our thinking. Labeling isn't important at this point; understanding is. You simply want to understand what truly exists. So don't allow yourself to fall into patterns of good/bad thinking that can limit what you need to do about the constraint.

Think carefully about the following two statements. How might they limit an organization from truly coming to grips with some constraint that has prevented that group from achieving its goals?

- Bill is the smartest guy ever doing this. We are so glad to have him! This is so good!
- Bill is the only guy who can do this; we are stuck without him. What would happen if we lost him? This is really bad.

The more information you can gather and the more insight gained about the kink in your hose, the better.

Take the time to get intimate with all aspects of your constraint, so you can perform the next step well.

Jim's process for identifying his kink in the hose began with his greatest pain point—his absence from home, missing his family and realizing his kids were growing up without him. He recognized that the growing success of the on-air program part of his business would only make things worse, since no one else in the company was doing the on-air job. Jim took great satisfaction in the results he achieved and in the sincere appreciation that regularly came his way, but he also recognized that preparing for the on-air portion of his job often required him to travel to foreign countries to help him better understand the needs of his clients. This required additional time away time from his family. Finally, Jim recognized that the reputation he had built over the years by doing this work had helped fuel new business and gave him a great deal of personal satisfaction. So while he considered the experience an energizing and rewarding journey, by now it had become a painful dilemma in which he felt trapped.

Jim's growing awareness of his problem fueled his intimacy with this kink in the hose. His wife's multiplying complaints that she felt like a single parent fueled his desire to spend more time with his family during this important life stage. Jim's first marriage had ended in divorce, and the pain sensitivity to his wife's needs vs. his business's needs sharpened his focus. Jim could easily see how much satisfaction he felt when he succeeded on the air, and how the praise he received for his work from multiple sources represented a powerful pull to continue past behavior. And so he felt stuck between a rock and a hard place. His growing company needed the revenue his work brought in, even though each business success seemed to increase the emotional pain that both he and his family felt.

3. **Cast a vision to picture the ideal future.** *

Never underestimate the power of the human imagination! Carefully ponder the following Sticky Leadership Axiom, one that I consider critical:

> *An inspiring vision, powerfully spoken, that be becomes shared, will pull for its own fulfillment.*

A clear and shared picture of an ideal future has staggering power. It aligns people's thinking, calls team members to engage and support, and provides clarity of a future outcome that you can use to direct your current actions. Sticky leaders who tap the power of vision know that crafting a detailed picture of the future is essential to converting an obstacle into a breakthrough. Without the clarity of a compelling future that everyone can buy into, you will have trouble focusing and applying your team's energy and resources.

The process of crafting a vision often involves understanding the current uncomfortable reality and flipping it to its opposite. So you may go from, "We have only one person who can do this, because these skills are hard to find," to "We have multiple people who can do this and we have discovered that many can do it."

That's essentially what happened with Jim's business. He recognized himself as the key constraint,

---

* For tools and help in creating an inspiring personal vision that can become shared go to: www.StickyLeadership.com/PersonalVision

as the only one in his company tasked to do the on-air radio work. The new vision he and his peers developed replaced the mindset of "Jim is the only expert talent we have who does our radio fund raising events" with "we have multiple people who can go on air all across the country, hosting successful fund raising programs for delighted clients."

This new vision called for hiring multiple on-air personalities, all as skilled as Jim, to simultaneously deliver the work to various clients. The breakthrough idea was to create a school of sorts where Jim could invite talented candidates to work on the team, even part-time. It took the company a little while to develop the new vision, but Jim and his colleagues persisted in looking for it and eventually found a great new solution.

Quite frankly, it has surprised me over the years to see how many problem-solving leaders lack the commitment it takes to stick with the visioning process. They fail to get detailed clarity about some desirable future because they want to jump at the first solution they dream up. They want to get busy right away—but in doing so, the "vision" they create lacks power and so fails to galvanize their people into the kind of focused action that can help the group remove its constraint and thereby get back on the road to achieving its goals. Sticky leaders know that the clarity required to design and cast an inspiring future is the very tool that will enable them and others to find the energy they need to Love Uphill in reaching their goal.

Think of the obstacles you now face and the apparent control they have over your thinking and your time. These obstacles are what keep you stuck. I find that struggling leaders often unwittingly create a guiding vision of exactly what they don't want—and it controls them. As you ponder your own obstacles, ask yourself how much "gravitational pull" they have on your thinking and on your time. The truth is, the more we talk about and dwell on something, whether positive or negative, the more real and tangible it becomes to us. We tend to believe that what exists now will tend to continue as it is, without realizing that our very thinking on the issue may cause it to remain so.

I compare such a focus of attention to gravity. The more we dwell on something, the more its gravity draws us into its orbit. And like gravity, the more massive the object, the more its gravitational pull. If you weighed 150 pounds on earth, for example, you would weigh 351 pounds on Jupiter, due to its vastly greater mass.

Now think about your business. The obvious current reality—what you see occurring right now—seems very real to you because it is taking place right in front of you. The more you focus on your difficult circumstances, the more real and powerful they become in how you think and act. Those circumstances pull you into their orbit through the force of gravity they exert. So the question then becomes, what can you do to change your future so that it doesn't look like your present?

If you want to change your future, then you have to create a clear and potent vision of what you want to see happen, an envisioned future with a mass at least as large as the picture of your current circumstances. You need a crystal clear vision with enough gravitational pull to draw everyone in your organization into its orbit. The more "real" something seems, the more gravitational pull it has on our thinking and actions. Visionary leaders therefore must have a way of making real the future they imagine, so that it has enough gravitational pull to attract the people and resources required to change the organization's current trajectory. This compelling vision is what pulls us to Love the Uphill work that's coming, the hard labor required if we are to reach our desired goals.

Without a clear picture of a compelling future—one that seems as real as the present—we will never achieve the escape velocity we need to leave behind the disappointments of the past and safely reach the fulfillment ahead. A sharply defined vision calls our minds, hearts and actions to the new possibility clearly pictured by our compelling vision.

I've helped hundreds of leaders create a detailed and inspiring picture of their future strong enough to replace an old vision whose gravity had them orbiting around persistent difficulties. The process is built around the idea that what is ultimately important about any vision is its foundation. The anchoring points are what I call "key commitment areas." For a personal vision, these commitment areas can be marriage, family, career, finances, health, learning, fun, or community. In business, I often hear of customers, profitability, quality products, meaningful work, innovation, or teamwork.

List your top key commitment areas by importance. Then select the first four and ask yourself, "If my dreams for this area of importance are fully realized in the best possible way, what would I see happening?" Imagine that you have a time machine and can dial yourself three years into the future. Grab your time travel cell phone, step into the time machine, and give me a phone call once you arrive. What do you see in the future? Describe it. Pay attention to what others are saying and how they appear to be thinking and feeling about this future reality.

This exercise provides a foundation for a detailed conversation about your envisioned future and helps you to capture it in narrative form. What passes for a vision statement often is nothing more than a mission statement; it lacks a detailed description of some desired future state. An effective vision statement must have enough detail to clearly describe what lives in your imagination. Others must be able to see what you see. Once you have the language for the vision, share it often with those who also need to imagine it.

Successful visionary leaders continually speak the vision, describing in detail the ideal future they see, over and over again. They want to make it tangible enough to compete with the current problems that argue for their people's attention, day in and day out. We all tend to get stuck in the present, and without being intentional about picturing some new and captivating future, we will almost certainly stay where we are (until gravity pulls us even lower).

If you want to break away from the status quo, then you need to start creating a picture of some alternate future that promises to deliver much more than you currently have. That future has to be realistic, of course, but also clear and detailed. It has to feel as real as your current situation.

This is far more than wishful thinking! Neuroscience tells us that the brain can't really tell the difference between some detailed, compelling picture of the future, and what it's currently experiencing. Both things tend to generate very similar kinds of chemical and electrical footprints.[1] Consider just one perspective on this recent research:

---

1 The Neuroscience of Your Brain on Fiction: http://nyti.ms/FSBPWr.

The brain, it seems, does not make much of a distinction between reading about (imagining) an experience and encountering it in real life; in each case, the same neurological regions are stimulated. Keith Oatley, an emeritus professor of cognitive psychology at the University of Toronto (and a published novelist), has proposed that reading produces a vivid simulation of reality, one that "runs on minds of readers just as computer simulations run on computers." Fiction—with its redolent details, imaginative metaphors and attentive descriptions of people and their actions—offers an especially rich replica. Indeed, in one respect novels go beyond simulating reality to give readers an experience unavailable off the page: the opportunity to enter fully into other people's thoughts and feelings.

When you create a compelling vision of the future for you and your colleagues, one that's both realistic and achievable, you create the kind of massive object that has the power to draw people from an old, decaying orbit into a new, vibrant one. And by continually speaking of that future and bringing it to life in the imaginations of your people, you set the stage for growth.

4. **Look for the dominant constraint that keeps your current reality from moving in the direction of the vision.**
The dominant constraint that keeps your current reality from moving toward the vision may be the same constraint that you identified in step one, but not necessarily. Consider Jim's story once again. Remember that the kink in the hose for his business was that his company had no one but him to serve as the on-air personality to lead its radio fundraisers, and the new solution was to create a sort of "school"

where suitable candidates could train to become just as proficient on-air as Jim. But what if, once Jim and his colleagues had created the new corporate vision, something else prevented that vision from taking hold in the imaginations of their colleagues? What if, let's say, a key manager kept saying, "We could never afford to hire and train new talent"? In that case, the dominant constraint standing in the way of the business moving toward the new vision would be the manager's opposition to the plan, not the original kink in the hose. A breakthrough helps you to get through the dominant obstacle and establish some forward momentum. And that changes everything.

To find the key constraint, ask the question: "What is the biggest, most difficult thing keeping us from moving toward the vision?"

In the beginning, breakthroughs often sound extravagant or even impossible. But this never thwarts sticky leaders. Their breakthrough thinking habits keep them asking good questions until they develop some vision that is both believable and attractive, a vision far better than the current reality. And then they look for whatever kinks in the hose keep their organization from moving toward that new, compelling vision.

5. **Develop a strategy to eliminate the constraint.**

Sticky leaders are smart about how things and people work. They know that the process of eliminating a constraint has to be simple to succeed. Therefore, they work hard to design a clever way of thinking about the obstacle holding them back from the work necessary to fulfill the vision. Sticky leaders know how to find leverage in circumstances by looking for what they want to see happen.

Look for what is keeping your available energy and resources from being successfully applied to create the results you desire. Good strategy involves both how you think about the obstacle and your attitude about it. You first have to believe that success is possible. Then you have to believe in the strategy you select—and the process of following that strategy must be simple enough that everyone can understand it. Consider the best, simple explanation of strategy I've ever heard: "Strategy is a way through difficulty."

A first grade teacher in a very poor school district, one with the lowest academic scores in the country, realized that her organizational kink in the hose had less to do with money (and the district had none, anyway) than it did with the attitude of her kids and their parents. She saw that both the children and the district battled an image that insisted the students weren't smart or capable of learning, that they could never overcome a host of handicaps brought on by poverty and lack of funding. So this entrepreneurial leader taught her kids what a scholar was, and then cleverly convinced the children that they were scholars. They went home and did the same for their parents, explaining what a scholar is and that they were scholars. By the end of the first year, these kids were reading at a third grade level. They had accomplished a remarkable breakthrough without receiving any additional school funds. All clever strategies follow that pattern: Simple, doable, and effective.

Sticky leadership strategy changes the thinking and actions of those involved, so that over time, together they make progress toward the vision. A good strategy causes us to think and act differently. In the example of the student/scholars, a new understanding of "scholar" changed their thinking and then their actions, which altered how they participated and thought about their capacity for learning.

6. **Apply the needed energy to work the strategy.**

Once you have a strategy, work it. View leadership as what you can do to close the gap between what is and what you want to be. This is where you apply your energy, creativity, and sustained effort, using your strategy, to cause something positive to happen.

One of the many things I admire about entrepreneurs is that they don't quit. If you want to create a breakthrough, you have to settle the issue up front that you will never give up. You will need to learn how to combine your own energy with that of others, and then sustainably use that combined, focused energy to create the results you want.

For sticky leaders, getting started on a breakthrough marks the beginning of that breakthrough. Where others just try harder, doing more of what they had been doing, sticky leaders get going with an inspiring vision that calls them and others to attack the dominant constraint. In that way, they build momentum that moves them in a new, more satisfying direction.

Keeping an Uphill Focus

Where are you looking? On what have you set your gaze? How do you feel about the picture you see? Our actions and our feelings tend to correlate with the thing on which we fix our eyes (and therefore what we see as our future). Launching the Uphill journey starts with identifying a breakthrough and becoming absolutely clear about what success looks like. I like to ask my coaching clients, "When it works, what does it look like?"

In Jim's story, the whole company began embracing the vision of multiple individuals capable of doing the on-air job. They successfully launched Host University and enrolled six talented and experienced radio personalities in the program. One exceptional participant soon agreed to come on board full time, and in the first few months, she looked like a star in the making. Shortly thereafter, however, family difficulties required her to resign from the business.

Jim felt both disappointed and frustrated. It seemed like a huge failure to him. For a time, the inspired vision seemed quite far off. Not surprisingly, the old one occasionally replaced the new one. Jim saw himself becoming the only on-air talent again, working a ridiculous number of hours and hurting his family through his prolonged and persistent absences.

But it's called "Loving Uphill," right? Expect such challenges. Starting the Uphill journey is just that, starting.

Jim had hoped to crest the hill quickly so he could begin coasting downhill. He envisioned having a number of on-air hosts, and for a short time, he actually lived his dream. But then life intervened and he had to start over, trying to find someone else he could train to take on the role of host.

When you're learning to Love Uphill, you often have to learn how to manage disappointment. Sticky leaders practice the discipline of staying focused on the desirable future, no matter what. Everything doesn't always work perfectly the first time around. In fact, it seldom does.

When you stick with it, though—when you keep focusing on the inspiring vision you've spoken and shared—that vision will pull for its own fulfillment. The broad smile that lights up Jim's face today powerfully reminds me of that truth.

FIND the ENERGY to SUSTAIN
the UPHILL JOURNEY

Does success in leadership sometimes seem like "last man standing?" We've all run into those dark periods when we think about giving up. We feel tired, worn out, frustrated, and it seems our best-laid plans are all failing. We feel like quitting.

What then?

Many of the entrepreneurial leaders I've worked with over the years have much at stake personally in launching and growing their companies. They often sign personal guarantees to borrow money from a bank. This means that everything they own backs up the loan. They have literally put it all on the line.

Have you ever sweated to make payroll? Many of my clients have. One of these leaders described to me how one day he crawled under his desk in tears, as if to hide from the fact that he didn't know how to make payroll the next day. When an unexpected check came in at the last minute, "Rick" received the funds he needed to get by for one more pay period.

Maybe you've flirted with the "short form bankruptcy" idea—just getting on a plane and leaving it all behind. But rarely is this an option, and it's never a good one. Succeeding in business usually requires a commitment to persevere, to endure, to hang on until the tide changes and your vision starts taking shape in the real world.

Rick, the entrepreneur I just mentioned, had the courage to hang on until one day, a Fortune 100 company offered him millions for his business. His destiny immediately reversed itself, in a magnificent way. While most stories lack such a grand finale, almost every kind of business success requires hanging in there, no matter what. It's a crucial part of Learning to Love Uphill. Sticky leaders trust that somehow things will work out. And so they continue to work hard, plan and persevere, in the process living to fight another day.

Of course, sheer energy and willpower won't suffice to achieve a successful breakthrough. None of us has unlimited energy. We can endure only for so long. Sticky leaders know that their edge lives in discovering the unique energy that they and others bring to their breakthroughs. Sticky leaders therefore realize that they need to be smart and strategic in how they use the differing kinds and amounts of energy they have on their teams. It turns out that each of us has varying amounts of four types of energy, combined in a unique array.

Everybody's Different

I have carefully studied people for more than two decades. I've learned that we are just like our fingerprints—no two of us are exactly alike. Our personal differences give us our strategic edge and provide clear reasons for not copying the successful leaders we admire.

Certainly, we ought to study and heed the counsel of other effective leaders. But as we do so, we must never forget that each of us has our own style, based on our unique differences.

Ultimately, we express our individual differences in the way we use our energy. I see understanding leadership energy as the key to sustainable leadership practices. Understanding leadership energy helps us to blend our willpower with our endurance so that we can achieve the breakthroughs we need.

Four Types of Leadership Energy

Over the years, psychologists have created a myriad human assessment instruments to help us know ourselves better. These instruments use various means to compare our similarities and differences and to assist us in speaking of them helpfully. These tools often get branded by letter codes or the name(s) of their inventors, or by the functions they are supposed to measure and quantify. You've probably heard of many of them, or used some of them, with names like DiSC and Meyers-Briggs and the Minnesota Multiphasic Personality Inventory (MMPI). Most of them seem to have one thing in common: They tend to measure four dimensions of how we use our energy.

Have you noticed that you use your energy most effectively when you operate within your core strength? Recent strengths-based research has demonstrated that we work most capably when we work from the core of our basic personalities. We are most effective as leaders when we are most ourselves. We also have more energy at our disposal when we work within our natural gifting, consistent with our basic nature and aligned with our unique design.

This means that comparing ourselves with others is not only unfair, it also can cause us serious problems. Foolish comparisons can prompt us to condemn ourselves on the one hand, or trick ourselves into believing we can do something that we probably never should have tried doing on the other.

Using the "four quadrants thinking" employed by many human assessment instruments, and considering the fact that we each have a unique array of ways to use our energy, allows us to make some keen observations about what actually works on the job.

COACHING CORNER

"In what type of leadership challenge
am I the most capable?"

*We each have unique capacity in some area.
Can you recognize yours?*

I've processed thousands of these human assessment instruments for all types of leaders, and have discovered that some of us have deep reserves in one or two of these quadrants, while others have a more even distribution across the four quadrants, but with lesser amounts in each. In other words, some of us have deep reserves in one particular area, but not much endurance in the other three, while some have a more even distribution, but lack the endurance of others in a particular area.

This fact becomes a huge clue to how we can make the best use of our energy. How can we act in strategically smart ways as leaders when we have to push things forward, even when it feels like an uphill slog? How can we sustain the momentum we need to keep moving forward?

There are essentially four types of leadership energy[2], and each of us has varying capacity or depth for each kind. Your leadership energy can be expressed in one of four basic ways:

- Relationship Building and Maintenance

- Problem Solving and Innovation

- Action and Results Building

- Information Collection and Stewardship

---

2 If you want to know more about leadership energy and receive a free assessment to learn more about yourself, go to www.StickyLeadership.com/EnergyAssessment

Although all of us have limits in regard to how we use our energy, for some reason we often misunderstand how much and what type of energy is required to obtain good results. Many leaders tend to assume that sheer willpower can compensate for any shortage or shortcoming in various energy types. It can't. Once you accept that each of us has limits in any of these four types of energy, the more skillful a leader you can become. Studying in more detail how our energy works provides crucial insight into how to improve our personal effectiveness and the effectiveness of our teams. Here is what I mean.

Each of us uses the four types of energy in certain recognizable patterns. Our capacity in each type, and even our thinking, is colored by our reserves for each type. All of us are wired naturally to have clear favorites.

Those with Relationship Building and Maintenance energy increase their supply when they interact with people, and lose energy when they work on projects alone. Don't think "introvert" or "extrovert" here, but rather about energy levels when dealing with people. Individuals with this kind of energy are great at initiating and preserving relationships. Someone with fewer reserves of this energy type loses whatever little he or she has during interactions with people, particularly with individuals unfamiliar to them. They need "alone time" to recharge their internal battery.

Problem Solving and Innovation energy allows individuals to solve problems and dream up creative solutions. People with rich energy reserves of this type thrive as inventors and often have new ideas to make life better. They have a passion to innovate with excellence. Others often view them as critical of outside ideas and they generally take longer to launch new initiatives because they overthink and unnecessarily complicate things. They often resist someone coming behind them to improve their work with better or fresher ideas. A person with low amounts of this energy isn't much of perfectionist and doesn't naturally care about accuracy. They have little patience for problem solving and will fail if given tricky problems to solve.

You can readily recognize those with the energy for Action and Results Building. They can be called pushy but earn appreciation for their bias toward action. People with this type of energy love making lists of things to do and enjoy getting tasks done. It seems like the more they get done, the more energy they have for doing whatever gets handed to them. They like coming up with processes and checklists. They often seem impatient and don't like being in meetings because they believe they could be doing more important things than sitting around and talking.

Those with the energy for Information Collection and Stewardship are skilled at taking care of what they have been given. They are committed to preserving the status quo or maintaining agreed upon standards. People with deep reserves of this energy like collecting data and information and always treat it as precious. They don't mind routine and repetitious tasks because they are able to master them that way. They love numbers and data and have a way of uncovering risk and protecting those around them by using that information. They become energized in their own quiet way with information and routine and seem to have endless methods of frustrating those who just want to get things done. It's as if they are in love with process and the written word and they can easily judge those who don't share their passion.

To become a sticky leader, you must be able to look strategically at any situation and determine the best type of leadership energy it requires. Whenever you face a leadership challenge of any kind, ask yourself a crucial question:

What type of energy does this situation call for, in this moment?

Of all the self-coaching questions sticky leaders can ask themselves, I believe this may be the most important of all. It can take many forms, of course, as in the following examples:

- "Do we need to strengthen or obtain relationships here?"
- "To move things forward, does this situation call for problem solving or innovation?"
- "Do I most need to take action and focus on results?"
- "Do I need to collect relevant facts to protect some aspect of what we are doing or what we have accumulated?"

Each of us has sufficient energy to initiate the next step in a breakthrough process. But if we need a sustained amount of energy in any one of these areas, over time, we must evaluate if we have sufficient reserves in that area to persevere until the situation requires a different type of leadership energy. Being able to self-assess what type of leadership energy we need, and then to determine our own capacity in that area, will inform our next moves as leaders working through to a breakthrough.

To assess what type of leadership energy we need, we have to get in relationship with the circumstance. And how do we do that? We work to understand it thoroughly and then identify the right kind of leadership energy required to solve it. Leaders who want to shift their current reality must accurately identify what is actually occurring and then identify the appropriate type of leadership energy required in that moment. When they do this, they gain influence over the situation. Those who do not understand this secret see what these leaders do and think, *Wow, magic!* It really is that potent.

You Can't Do It All Yourself

How many times have you said to yourself, "Why can't these people just get it? I guess I'll just have to do this on my own"?

Or maybe you've said under your breath, "This is too much work to hand off to someone else. I guess I need to do it all myself."

On the one hand, choosing to do the task yourself will reinforce your leadership position (everyone knows you are the leader because you take charge and make things happen). But on the other hand, when you do this again and again, what message are you sending to your team members? You'll be like the mom who keeps telling her son to clean up his room, and when he doesn't, in exasperation she gets frustrated and does it herself. The kid knows that if he just waits long enough, Mom will do it and he won't have to.

Everyone is watching you, the leader, for clues about how to act. Your people want to please you, so they watch both what you say and what you do, and then they use that information to guide their actions. Leaders who take everything on themselves, especially when circumstances get difficult, unwittingly train those around them to depend on them in very unhealthy ways. In the leadership game, actions always speak louder than words. So if you are asking people to step up and take responsibility, but then grab it yourself for any number of reasons, you are reinforcing their unhealthy dependence on you.

And that puts you squarely in the role of constraint. You have now become the kink in the hose that holds back your business. Rather than follow such an unproductive course, learn how to recognize the energy available on your team and then put it to work. Trying to do everything yourself will inevitably lead to leadership burnout.

I often get called in when such a sequence of events has become engrained in an organization. Inevitably, the leader has become worn out and frustrated and begins to angrily judge his people as uncommitted or incapable. Some individuals may, in fact, be uncommitted or incapable; but in many cases, these leaders have never even tested their staff members to see if they have what it takes, because they keep taking back the leadership authority they say they so desperately want to hand off. In such cases, the real truth is very hard to come by.

Leaders who get stuck in this trap wind up in a vicious cycle. The leader gets enthroned in a patriarchal or parental role, co-workers behave like misbehaving little kids, and frustration mounts on all sides. Capable leaders within the ranks become frustrated because although they have been asked to "step up," they get slapped down every time they try.

Can you begin to see how this process leads to unsustainable leadership? The leader in charge will burn out, often due to limited capacity in one or more of the four energy quadrants. So the leader runs out of gas, due to a lack of sufficient energy to handle whatever the circumstances require in that moment.

I once had a client who had enjoyed a very successful career in the high tech industry. "Fred" then decided to build his own company by purchasing a franchise that required a significant amount of leadership energy in the relationship building and maintenance quadrant. The problem is that he had built his career around his strengths of using and protecting information. Fred got things done by moving people into action with the facts, by marshaling the truth of the circumstances. He had very little capacity in the relationship building and maintenance quadrant.

So when Fred grew frustrated or pressed by his circumstances, guess what he did? He began using information as a blunt instrument, challenging his people to get into action by using data, the quadrant where he had real depth as a leader. But because he didn't even recognize the need for building relationships and truly connecting with his people, his attempts to bludgeon them into action with the facts often got misunderstood and created mountains of frustration. Significant numbers of his people felt threatened and eventually quit.

You can probably see why personnel turnover often afflicts organizations like this. As people get frustrated and feel misunderstood, they quit; and then the leader often feels at wits end and near burnout himself, as he continues to get challenged beyond his capacity. Even worse, through his overuse of actions associated with his favorite data quadrants, he continues to burn much of his leadership energy in unproductive ways.

So what's the solution to such a dilemma? It's quite simple, actually. Sticky leaders learn how to apply the appropriate leadership energy right for the moment.

A Two-part Process

The sticky leadership solution utilizes a two-part process.

1. Know the energy required to succeed in the process of leadership.

2. Assemble a smart team to sustainably achieve the end result, over time.

First, sticky leaders work to become keenly aware of what kind of energy the situation requires, in the moment. When it calls for building and maintaining relationships, that's the kind of leadership energy they must use to influence the circumstances. They know that other types of energy simply will not work.

Think of having a lock that calls for a certain type of key. Only one key will unlock the breakthrough you need in that moment, in those circumstances.

Sticky leaders learn to recognize which of the four types of energy are called for in any given situation, and then they use that kind of energy, regardless of the depth or shallowness of their own resources of it. Fred learned over time to use his relationship building and maintenance energy when required, even though he didn't have much depth in that energy quadrant. He had to learn how to be strategic in how he used his limited resources in that area.

Applying the appropriate energy to specific circumstances begins to engage people immediately and gets things moving in the right direction. As a result, sticky leaders bring powerful leverage to moving the obstacle or constraint.

Second, sticky leaders learn how to build smart teams and then use them strategically. They know that a big part of their job is to share the leadership load with gifted leaders around them. To be a sticky leader requires that you develop the leadership skills of your associates by teaching and modeling the principles of sticky leadership, and then inviting them to participate in the leadership task. Co-workers always learn more by observation and experience than by getting lectures or hearing sermons. Remember that your people are watching you, and your actions speak louder than words. When your words both coordinate and reinforce your actions, you create a very potent leadership matrix.

Building smart energy teams requires that you understand your fellow leaders on the team and have a good sense of their own leadership energy. Remember, each of us feels most comfortable and capable in the energy quadrants where we have the greatest capacity. Therefore as a leader, it is important to give leadership opportunities to others who have whatever kind of energy a situation demands at the time.

Once more, consider Fred, the leader who didn't have natural depth in the relationship building and maintenance quadrant. Eventually he learned who on his team had more relationship energy than him, and he began to "toss the ball" to these team members when the amount of energy required outstripped his own capacity. He often started some initiative and then handed it off to someone else with more capacity in the relationship energy quadrant. In that way, he learned to sustain the hard work of Loving Uphill.

If you want to create resilient and sustainable leadership, that's how you must do it. You have to think more "team" than "me," because none of us has unlimited capacity in all four quadrants. It's foolish, and sometimes catastrophic, to expect that circumstances will always align with the unique array of energy any one of us has available.

Smart energy teams know about and accept the energy capacity of each team member. They know how to step in when needed to help another leader who got things started, but who needs more energy of a type other than what he or she has available. This requires a willingness to be transparent and honest about personal strengths and weaknesses. Sticky leaders can talk about these issues and appreciate one another for their differences.

In one sense, what happens is a "transfer of leadership energy." The whole becomes greater than the sum of its parts. Smart energy leaders constantly gauge the available leadership energy on their team and look to add other members to the team who bring other kinds of energy needed to strengthen the team's overall capacity. Then by "passing the ball" to the person with the needed kind of energy, other team leaders have the opportunity to learn and grow their own leadership skills.

Sticky leaders who learn to wisely utilize their own energy, and who know the energy profiles of their team members and who have learned how to appropriately marshal them, become both confident and capable of taking the right action. They know they can't do it all by themselves. But they also know that whether the challenge concerns relationships, problem-solving or innovation, getting people to take action, or honoring data and being good stewards of key information, they have the skills on their team to achieve the goals they all have in their sights.

Problems: The Fuel for Sticky Leaders' Energy

What is your first reaction when new problems arise? Particularly the ones you didn't see coming?

Very likely, you're like most of us when we have to deal with problems. You would rather they not exist. But when they come, how do you usually react? Be honest now, and put a check in the box below that best describes your normal reaction to problems:

❑ I resist them.
❑ I complain about them.
❑ I initially get disappointed by them.
❑ I look for more information about them.
❑ I get angry with the person bringing them.
❑ I embrace them.

The majority of us probably vote for one of the first three responses. I used to think that this leadership thing wouldn't be half bad if it weren't for the problems that came with it. For me, the problems most often showed up in the form of people. But think for a moment about what that statement actually means. It's essentially like saying, "Driving my car would be way more fun if no other drivers got on the road." Accurate, maybe, but not very realistic. Some among us may actually find it more fun and challenging to drive while surrounded by platoons of cars, but most of us don't. We'd prefer a much less taxing environment.

The truth is, sticky leaders have a unique relationship with problems. They have an unusual ability to embrace problems rather than resist them or complain about them. It isn't that they feel complacent about issues; in fact, sticky leaders aggressively pursue problems and use their ability to convert obstacles to breakthroughs—with a vengeance. They've learned to become realists about the problems they face. They know that problems always come with the leadership territory. For them, problems are very much the fuel that supplies their Uphill energy.

So what should you do if this "bring on the problems" perspective doesn't naturally come to you? Do you just try to convince yourself that whenever problems appear, you must pause and think differently? Is it purely a mental exercise?

While sticky leaders do sometimes have to retrain their brains to think differently, the "realist" part of becoming a sticky leader goes a bit further. To be totally honest with the circumstances and with ourselves, sticky leaders have to recognize the following truths:

- **Most opportunities, visions, and possibilities don't happen automatically.**

  It takes energy to bring forth the majority of these new, wonderful things. An ideal future will come into existence only when the problems that hold it back from making its appearance are identified and get converted to new outcomes, aligned with the vision or possibility. This is at the heart of what sticky leaders do.

- **By definition, we act to change the current course of events.**

  Sticky leaders make things happen that otherwise would never occur. But inertia does not bend to the momentum of thoughts only; sticky leaders must apply their willpower, expressed in the use of appropriate leadership energy, to change the course of those events.

- **We will have to do things we've never done before.**

  When we begin to invest ourselves in bringing a vision into reality, to create something new that didn't exist before, we must admit that we are stepping into the unknown. We must embrace the learning lessons that come with the adventure. We learn by doing, by going through the process of taking the best action we know how to take, by addressing each problem and challenge as it comes. We see these problems as learning opportunities that will, over time, strengthen our leadership ability. This is not only inevitable, but also valuable.

Sticky leaders feel most alive and energized and fully engaged when they work from their learning edges. This is not a place in the safe center of what they already know they can do! Instead, it presses the envelope of their learning and sends them to a place where they expose themselves to new lessons and strange experiences that cause them to grow. Sticky leaders don't resent this, but rather learn to embrace it.

- **Valuable does not always equal fun or easy.**

Sticky leaders are value driven. They seek to create value and they live and operate by their values. They know that locked in each problem is a valuable discovery, product, lesson, or intermediate outcome that can be released only by tackling the problem head-on. They are like miners, looking for the vein of gold in a wall of rock, willing to put forth the effort to bring out hidden value from the matrix of current hard reality. Sticky leaders become skilled at bringing value to any situation, even when it seems difficult to see in the beginning, and even when it takes time to reveal itself.

Use Energy to Gain Leverage

While I strongly believe everything I just wrote, the truth is that problems can indeed wear us down and overcome us . . . if we don't tackle them in a smart and strategic way. Remember that each of us has a limited amount of leadership energy in each quadrant, and for most of us, problems seem to consume a big portion of that energy.

In my experience, nearly all of us find a problem energizing in the beginning. If the problem shows no sign of budging, however, or if it extends over a longer period than we expected, we run the risk of compromising our objectives or folding in the face of this stubborn obstacle. Some problems are quite capable of outlasting us, and thus threaten to prevent us from turning an obstacle into a breakthrough. Sticky leaders, therefore, learn how to size up problems, cut them into pieces, and then hand them over to other leaders who can crack open the stubborn pieces of rock to reveal the gold inside. This divide-and-conquer thinking naturally organizes itself into three parts:

1. Determine the leadership capacity you have available.

2. Break the problem down into logical parts, based on the type of energy needed to solve each part.

3. Match the people we have available to the different parts, based on their capacity in whatever energy type is required to solve each part.

The best way to proceed, therefore, is to use the distinctions identified earlier about the four energy types. Each of us has some amount of leadership energy available. We each have a unique array of leadership capacity, defined by varying amounts of the four main types of leadership energy:

- Relationship development and maintenance
- Problem solving and innovation
- Action and driving results
- Honoring information and stewarding data.

The first step is to recognize the capacity we have at our disposal. Sticky leaders recognize other "leaders within the ranks." Because we view leadership not as a hierarchical position but as a role anyone can play when acting on their true commitments, we have an expanded view of those who can help us convert problems into things of real value. When we look for those who are committed to the vision, solution or possibility we want to bring forth, we begin to see leaders all around us. We can create a team of leaders by taking the time to become familiar with their specific energy distributions.

You could think of this as recognizing the leadership strengths of others, but it's really more than that. You want to identify both the leadership potential and the capacity of these leaders. That isn't always easy, but your ability to identify the leadership portfolio of others will become extremely valuable once you start embracing problems and converting them to visions. You'll see that such conversations happen most easily once you release the potential of your leaders by tapping their energy strengths. You can do this by asking a series of questions and categorizing each leader on your team by using the following criteria:[3]

1. Among the four types of leadership energy, which is this person's most favorite? In other words, what do they do best?

   a. Relationship building and maintenance
   b. Problem solving and innovation
   c. Getting things done, moving others into action
   d. Honoring and using information and stewarding what they have.

2. Of the four types of leadership energy, what is their second most favorite? Others can easily recognize and access the top two types of leadership energy in nearly all of us.

---

3   V2A has more detailed tools to help you in this area. Contact V2A to discover the resources we can provide. www.V2A.com

3. Does this person like to lead and take charge on his/her own, or does this leader like to work on a team, strengthening the whole and supporting others?

4. How would this person respond to being asked to take on part of the problem?

5. If this person does take on part of the problem, what type of support would he/she want and need to succeed?

The second step is to divide a problem into its constituent parts, based the four ways leaders use their energy. Different parts of the problem require different kinds of leadership energy, just as different parts of creating a cake require different skills.

The third step is to match people to the right work based on the energy required to do the work well. The person who's good at finding bargains at the grocery store might not be the best at combining ingredients into a tasty batter! Your task as the leader is to break down the problem, based on the kinds of energy required to release the hidden value in each part.

Once you become familiar with the four types of leadership energy and can recognize each type in others, it becomes easier to see problems as puzzles made up of various parts, with each part most susceptible to a particular kind of energy. This is a skill that anyone can develop.

For sticky leaders, parsing a problem to be shared is a bit different than the way most people think about solving a problem. When you can give part of a problem to someone who has the right energy to solve it, that problem pops open like a coconut, struck in just the right place. Meanwhile, the rest of us stare on in amazement.

While sticky leaders focus on solutions, they also recognize that some problems may not have ready solutions. Instead, working on those problems leads to some valuable discoveries or to ideas for helpful next steps that no one could foresee before tackling the problem.

Dividing a problem into its constituent parts and handing off the parts to other leaders can help you create the breakthrough you need. Even better, that process also creates momentum, all by itself. Who has the right energy to extract value from each part of the problem? That's the key to finding your breakthrough. And it can actually become fun!

Think of a time when biking uphill seemed easy to you. What took place that made it seem as if you could go on forever? There is something to be said for finding your rhythm and getting into a groove as you pedal uphill. Although you know you are expending a lot of energy, something about conquering the hill shifts your perspective and you feel good about what you are doing and how it is going. It becomes fun, in a grueling sort of way.

Now mentally shift to your business obstacle. Imagine that you and everyone else working on the constraint feels just like the biker about to crest a monster hill. Can you imagine what that might feel like? This is the experience that sticky leaders dream of, something that inspires them to give their best and to bring others along on the arduous but fulfilling Uphill journey. This is what it feels like to convert an obstacle into a breakthrough.

What if You Lose Momentum?

Once an obstacle gets divided into its parts and each piece goes to the leader best suited to unlock the value in each part, team energy flows and good things start happening. You're moving uphill. Your breakthrough has begun. Everyone focuses on the vision and it's just a matter of time until current reality gives way to the new reality pictured by the vision.

But remember that this is a step-by-step process; it doesn't happen all at once.

During this phase, the sticky leader knows that despite the awesome feeling of progress and despite the euphoria of climbing the hill, times will almost certainly come when the team loses momentum and what once looked pretty easy starts looking very hard.

What to do then? You must find a way to regain your momentum and get back to pursuing the vision. Fortunately, sticky leaders have some potent tools that enable them to do exactly that.

SIX PRACTICES to INCREASE MOMENTUM

Not every good idea works. Sometimes, our best efforts fall short. On the best of teams, good people can communicate in unskillful ways that end up hurting one another. All of these unfortunate things can conspire to bring a halt to our Uphill momentum.

What happens then?

Sticky leaders know how to encourage the members of their teams by working from both the head and the heart. In so doing, they help everyone to work together once more to achieve the goal they all see clearly pictured in the vision.

No doubt you've heard someone say, "Well, his heart just wasn't in it," when describing how somebody gave up or quit on a project or idea. There's more truth to that statement than we might suspect! Our hearts are fickle and at times they faint in the grind of hard, Uphill work—even before the person runs out of willpower. As logical beings, we all know that nearly every problem can either be solved or navigated around, given enough time; but when our hearts lose interest, our wills often lose their determination to "just keep going."

This is why sticky leaders learn how to attend to the heart, with an eye toward recapturing the energy needed to finish the remaining Uphill work. When the going gets tough, the tough attend to the heart first, and only then to the head. When both the heart and head get engaged, any team can find the energy required to continue the sometimes arduous work of pedaling Uphill.

That Uphill work involves six practices that help sticky leaders to increase momentum or to restore lost momentum. Each of the six has both a heart and a head component.

One: Find What Works

We all get stalled on the Uphill climb in many ways, but things often slow down when an idea or plan ceases to work as we had hoped. Let's face it, when leaders set out to make something new happen, they are stepping into the unknown. Even though we work with "live ammo" in our efforts to move current reality toward some shared vision, we will have misfires, along with direct hits. While we can usually find something that's working, we also typically find something that isn't working or that needs to work better. For some reason, the "not working" part often drowns out what is working, and therefore has a major impact on our thinking and emotions.

Although it helps to remember that we have gifted leaders engaged in creating a breakthrough by focusing on various parts of the obstacle, that confidence-builder and leverage-provider does not guarantee success. And there always seem to be times when a member of the Uphill team gets asked to help out in an area where his or her energy and the assigned work don't perfectly align—and in those cases, we can expect that the work will seem more difficult than normal, often increasing the risk of failure or burnout.

So what fundamental concept can sticky leadership offer to help us find what works? When breakdowns happen in the journey to accomplishing a breakthrough, it is important to first focus on what worked, rather than on what didn't. Even though this is both logically (head) and emotionally (heart) intelligent, in my experience, I can tell you that it almost always seems counter intuitive. Although I can't explain why, human nature almost inevitably focuses first on what isn't working, a tack that really moves us in the wrong direction. Maybe in our early years at school, we learned to speak only if we had the right answer; and if we spoke anyway, perhaps we got publicly corrected, which taught us to obsess on fixing our errors rather than noticing what we got right. Or maybe our culture has so glorified problem-solving that it minimizes successful accomplishing. I'm not sure, but I doubt it much matters.

The truth is that keeping our hearts encouraged is closely tied to recognizing what's working well and knowing that, at some level, the desires of our hearts for forward progress is being met (if even in small ways). Keeping in mind what has worked keeps us hopeful of eventual success—and hope is a heart function, not a head function. When we lose heart, the Uphill journey begins to look impossible and hope begins to fade.

From a logical standpoint, we can always find something that seems to be working, a victory that we can celebrate and figure out how to leverage. We build momentum from continually investing our energy into leveraging what is working, rather than pouring massive amounts of energy into what hasn't and isn't working.

As an executive coach, I have had some remarkable successes using this principle to turn around clients perceived to be failing massively. Think of a key employee whose work is judged to be only twenty percent effective. This means a full eighty percent of her work is considered a failure. And don't kid yourself; if she has received honest feedback, she knows she is failing. We might make the logical assessment that all hope is lost for such a person. I've seen bosses at their wits' end who have told me, "Larry, if you can't help this person turn this around, she will be let go."

No pressure!

So where do I begin with someone who knows his or her job future is hanging by a thread? Do I begin by focusing on the eighty percent where everyone sees clear failure? That's generally what the boss already has done, and it hasn't worked. I know this, because that's how I got there. That's when "Last chance Larry" got called in.

Instead, I begin coaching such a demoralized client by itemizing what is working and where she is having success. Often I learn that what she has been given to do doesn't align with her leadership energy. Her strengths don't connect with the job expectations. But regardless of whether that's true, if the employee wants to keep her job, she needs an improvement in performance.

I find it helpful to look at the situation like this: The coaching client has only a twenty percent success platform on which to stand, and from that small piece of solid ground, the person has to take on the eighty percent that isn't working. Does it seem logical to think that by standing on the twenty percent that is working, she could leverage and change the entire eighty percent that isn't? Not very likely—and yet, that's often exactly what we do. Of course, we don't tackle the whole eighty percent at once! Instead, we stand on the solid twenty percent to tackle a failing twenty percent (one fifth of what isn't working).

It does make sense that with the twenty percent that's already working, I can leverage another twenty percent toward success. This takes smart focus. And then, looking at the entirety of what isn't working, we can find a portion of what remains to target what we can most easily tackle next.

In other words, we start with something easy and leave the hard parts to later.

By using such an incremental approach, we can anticipate that the targeted twenty percent can also be converted to solid working ground; and then we'll have forty percent working, with sixty percent failing. The boss of my theoretical client probably would still say, "Over half of what I'm expecting from her is not working," and that's true; but we aren't done yet.

Now we return to the Uphill challenge with increased leverage. Forty percent is now working, and in the coaching conversation, we target another forty percent (now the majority portion of what remains). Again, finding some momentum by increasing what is working, and using the forty percent to target another forty percent, is a fair and logical approach to improvement. This gives us a doable approach to expanding our acreage of working land.

Finally, when we succeed here, we can now stand on the eighty percent of what is working, leaving only twenty percent left. To be frank, the remaining twenty percent is probably the most difficult to tackle; but we now have a leverage advantage. We can apply the eighty percent of what is working to the twenty percent that still is not.

Sticky leaders use the same kind of incremental thinking to help a team of leaders gain momentum as they work Uphill to a breakthrough. They use smart leverage to incrementally help the team move forward. By focusing on what is working, we target the heart and bring hope when the odds seem so against us. In time, we can succeed. Sticky leaders have a saying:

Inch by inch, anything is a cinch.

Two: Loving Uphill Is All about Learning

Do you enjoy learning? Whenever I ask this question, and I do so often, a majority of adults tend to respond, "yes." In practice, however, I find that when the Uphill work gets hard, we tend to forget that we like learning new things.

Why is that?

Maybe it's because of the pressure we feel. Or it could be

the fear of letting others down. Maybe we are selective in what we like to learn, and since this difficult situation doesn't hold any excitement for us, we don't much care about any lesson it may want to teach us.

The truth is that breakthroughs always involve the unknown. We need to remember that we will get pushed to our learning edges. We learn leadership best through experience, not merely from a book (although books can help!). We learn best by watching effective leaders at work.

Sticky leaders have learned to embrace the lessons, even the ones they don't particularly want. The lessons coming at you right now have shown up to provide you with a new opportunity to learn and grow.

Learning begins in our mind, with an attitude of openness to learning what we don't already know. The press is full of stories about high-level leaders whose massive failures were caused largely by a lack of learning humility. The belief that, "I know what I'm doing and I'm not open to any other ideas. It's my way or the highway," is dangerous to both the leader and to those around them. In fact, such a rejection of learning causes us to repeat old patterns from the center of our leadership competency, based only on past success (what I call our leadership footprint), rather than from our learning edges and the new information that launches us into the unknown.

You might call such a defective perspective "the Maginot Line mentality." Remember the Maginot Line, the expensive border defenses that France constructed after World War I? The French wanted to make sure that Germany could never again threaten her military forces. But the massive border defenses the nation built, based on past combat strategy, proved spectacularly irrelevant when Hitler unleashed his blitzkrieg at the beginning of World War II. He simply went around them. And France fell to the Nazis in about six weeks.

Part of Learning to Love Uphill is learning to love learning, even when the lessons feel painful or embarrassing. All great leaders, if asked, will describe their greatest failures (probably with a great deal of relish), and then tell you how those failures helped them to achieve success.

Three: Managing Our Thinking

How we think impacts how life shows up. Each of us has a "world view" and this world view filters our experiences and therefore how each of us experiences life. Two people can observe the very same thing and yet report it quite differently. Why does this happen? World view. The frame through which we see and experience circumstances shapes our actions.

And how does this insight impact our Learning to Love Uphill? Our thinking frames our outlook, our outlook impacts our feelings, and in turn, our feelings animate our actions. Ultimately, how we think controls what we can do as leaders. One of the leadership experts I admire calls it TFA.[4] Our Thoughts direct our Feelings and our feelings control our Actions—T→F→A—therefore, our thoughts ultimately control our actions.

So how can we use this concept when we face Uphill work? This is the logical companion to the earlier section about taking care of our heart. When I'm with a client, I can't initially tell whether her heart or her head leads in reestablishing momentum after she got stalled in their Uphill climb. Some of us tend to be logic-driven while others tend to be emotion-driven. So each of us must answer the question on our own terms; and to be safe, I work on both approaches simultaneously. First, I attend to my heart and to the hearts of others; and then I use logic and pay careful attention to thinking and managing thoughts.

4   Ford Taylor, Transformational Leadership

Thoughts become real things when we honor them, the very process at work when we say, "An inspiring vision, powerfully spoken, that becomes shared, will pull for its own fulfillment." The power of a compelling vision and its capacity to pull toward itself everything it needs for fulfillment, lives in the power of human thought and what individuals spend their time thinking about.

"An inspiring vision, powerfully spoken, that becomes shared, will pull for its own fulfillment."

The thinking that lives and grows in our minds tends to become real over time. It's as if the fresh, green shoots of flexible new thoughts eventually turn into the hardwood of certainty. That process tends to channel our actions.

Henry Ford is recognized as one of the great early leaders of the industrial revolution, a man who eventually helped transform life into what we know today. He pioneered the manufacturing age and had much to say about leadership. One of his most oft-quoted sayings insists, "Whether you think you can do a thing or think you can't do a thing, you're right."[5]

So how does a sticky leader take responsibility for thinking and its impact on accomplishing some breakthrough? Six key questions point to the answer:

1. "Is the way we are thinking right now helping us or hurting us to move forward, now that things have become difficult?"

2. "Why are we thinking in this way?"

3. "How true is the information supporting this thinking, and why are we looking at the facts in this way?"

---

5 http://www.brainyquote.com/quotes/quotes/h/henryford122817. html#yRsGrLOlWvU5LEar.99

4. "Given the facts we have available and believe are true, is there an equally valid way of thinking that would be more helpful in moving us forward?"

5. "What prevents us from believing this new way, as opposed to the old way that has us stalled?"

6. "Who is willing to believe with us in this new way of thinking, and how can we encourage them to share it as widely as possible?"

This process has nothing to do with trying to lie to yourself to see if you can force your mind to think differently than it does. We are wired to sniff out lies. Our brains think logically and won't easily allow this sort of faulty processing. To move ahead, we have to find a logical argument that seems just as plausible as the one we currently hold, and then choose the equally valid but more helpful way of thinking. This process lies at the heart of our ability to break through obstacles when we get stalled. We change our minds to change our life.

Four: Quitting Is Not an Option

After all is said and done, at some point we have to decide that we just won't quit. In leadership, there is something about being "the last man standing." Perseverance and resilience go hand in hand. Each of us has our own willpower limits, and often when things get really stacked against us, we have to find a way to keep going beyond anything we initially thought possible. When you reach your limit and just know you can't go on, get up and go on for no other reason than that you know you can't quit.

Again and again, I have seen clients demonstrate that resilience means just getting up and doing the next right thing. When you don't know what to do next, ask yourself, "What would be the next right thing to do?" and just do that. Circumstances seem to change and move when we give them no other option.

You've probably heard the old story about Spanish explorer Hernando Cortez. When he landed in Mexico, he and his soldiers found themselves seriously outnumbered. Cortez, however, had a deep commitment to his mission and therefore commanded his men to burn their ships. In that way, they had only one choice: Win or die. Cortez acted strategically, not recklessly. He commanded his men to burn the boats, not to destroy all of their supplies and food. Good strategy is about closing off unacceptable options and eliminating excuses in order to focus all energy on overcoming the obstacle and achieving the breakthrough.

I remember when I started my consulting practice after a very successful software career. I had become a vice president at my company, helping to take it public. As a result, I'd made some good money. When I privately announced to my boss, the CEO and a man I trusted deeply, that I was planning to leave and start my own consulting firm, he gave his blessing. Months later, on the appointed day, I made a grand announcement of my transition and the company hosted a wonderful going away ceremony to acknowledge my ten years of service. It felt wonderful.

The next week, I "hung out my shingle" and began pursuing clients and building my practice. It was much harder than I thought, and at times scary. My wife was a stay-at-home mom, so the family depended completely on my income. I had saved some money for this occasion, but I still felt foolish and fearful at times when things did not go as well or develop as fast as I had planned.

On some days, I wondered whether my old company might take me back; but shortly after, I realized the obvious, that it already had filled my old position with someone better than me. There would be no returning to the old comfort of a former job! For me, that was the "burning the ships" event that would refocus me on what lay ahead, rather than pondering escape routes for a return to the past. It took me a full three years to arrive at the income I had achieved when I left my former company, so my Uphill journey took me much longer than I had planned.

As I look back, however, I feel tremendously grateful that I persisted. Today I enjoy my dream job and delight in the opportunity to help others live their own dreams.

Five: Taking Turns

By definition, a breakthrough is something significant that brings an inspiring vision into reality. This means it goes beyond anything a single person can do on his or her own. It takes working together, each leader doing his or her part.

And how do you pull together the right people to make the breakthrough happen? You share the vision and see who wants to be a part of it. Remember, "An inspiring vision, powerfully spoken, that becomes shared, will pull for its own fulfillment."

Still, even when you align everyone with the parts of the breakthrough that best match their leadership energy, times come when we all get stuck, tired, or just need to step back for a bit from the hard work of the Uphill climb. At these times, it's critical to take turns doing the hard work.

Years ago, a popular message made the rounds about why geese fly south in the customary V formation. The old story well describes the value and importance of working together and sharing the hard work:

Next fall, when you see Geese heading south for the winter, flying along in their customary V formation, you might consider what science has discovered as to why they fly that way. As each bird flaps its wings, it creates an uplift for the bird immediately following. By flying in V formation, the whole flock can go at least 71 percent further than if each bird flew on its own.

People who share a common direction and sense of community can get where they are going more quickly and easily because they are traveling on the thrust of one another.

When a goose falls out of formation, it suddenly feels the drag and resistance of trying to go it alone and quickly gets back into formation to take advantage of the lifting power of the bird in front.

If we have as much sense as a goose, we will stay in formation with those who are headed the same way we are.

When the Head Goose gets tired, it rotates back in the wing and another goose flies point.

It makes sense to take turns doing the hard jobs with people or with geese flying South.

Geese honk from behind to encourage those up front to keep up their speed.

What do we say when we honk from behind?

Now get this, and this is important, when a goose gets sick or is wounded by gunshots and falls out of formation, two other geese fall out with that goose and follow it down to lend help and protection. They stay with the fallen goose until it is able to fly, or until it dies. Only then do they launch out on their own, or with another formation to catch up with their group.

If we have the sense of a goose, we will stand by each other like that.

. . . .

Consider a few important ways to ensure that you take advantage of working together as a group:

- When you initiate an Uphill journey, have everyone agree that you will work together to share the load and stress. There is no shame in asking for help!

- Be attentive to others and watch for signs that they may want and need help. Offer it without being asked.

- Develop a level of candor and communication that can build trust and safety. Give permission to everyone to speak up when they have support needs.

- When people step in for you to carry the load for a period of time, make sure that you express your appreciation. Make reciprocity a practice among your group. What goes around comes around. Don't be afraid to pay it forward!

Six: Coaching and Encouragement

While encouraging your heart is an important dimension of Learning to Love Uphill, equally important is coaching and encouraging others. When everything else fails, resort to encouragement.

Some of us don't come by encouragement naturally. Fortunately, it's a skill that anyone can develop. If you're just innately wired to encourage others, go ahead and skip this section, knowing that what you do naturally is essential for Learning to Love Uphill. If you need a bit of encouragement to become an encourager, however, then allow me to relate a story from my early years as an executive coach.

Randy, the CEO I mentioned earlier who launched his own dental equipment company, hired me to coach him. He impressed me from the beginning, as he let me know in our very first meeting that his previous consultant had not worked out. I'll never forget him leaning forward and saying, "If this doesn't get more fun, I'm out of here."

Once he removed some of the early "kinks in the hose," Randy's business took off and he discovered that he needed to develop his leadership skills to complement his natural talents in product innovation and marketing. This was to be our focus. Randy wanted to find a way to enjoy his work while making the transition to becoming an executive capable of attracting, retaining, and leading people who could take his business to even greater levels of success. He also wanted to keep up with the changing needs of his target market.

Early on, Randy impressed me with his passion for product innovation and for meeting the needs of his customers. He struggled, however, in the area of leading his people and developing the business processes that would support the growing demand for his firm's products. I also noticed that Randy clearly cared for his people, something they all recognized—even in the face of his clumsy and sometimes angry expressions of frustration at their inability to make things work as he envisioned. In fact, many times I saw in the faces of his people a deep conflict between their recognition that despite his care for them, some of his approaches to overcoming an obstacle caused them a great deal of unnecessary pain.

In a coaching session one day, I decided to confront Randy with a puzzling observation I had made. I had seen him repeatedly shoot himself in the foot by the way he treated his people, particularly at critical times in their Uphill challenges. Although he was never abusive, he clearly lacked the ability to maintain a good connection with his people when things got difficult for everybody.

"Randy," I said, "I can tell that you really care about your people, and they know it. Still, I've never seen you compliment them or tell them they are doing a good job. And yet you never miss an opportunity to point out what they're doing wrong. Why is that?"

"Larry," he replied, "my dad was an alcoholic and he never gave me a compliment. I never heard once that he recognized anything I was doing as good. I could never please him and so I worked all the harder trying to do so."

I nodded and then said, "So you think that if you compliment your people or let them know you feel pleased with them, you're afraid they will quit working hard?"

"Exactly," he answered.

"I see," I said. "So then, Randy, let me ask you this. If your dad had complimented you and let you know how proud of you he was, would you have stopped working hard to try to please him?"

I immediately got the classic "deer in the headlights" stare. Randy sat quiet for what seemed like an eternity. He finally replied, softly, "No. I would not have stopped trying to please him."

"So here is the thing," I continued. "Why don't you try complimenting and letting your people know how you recognize their hard work and how much you really do appreciate them—and just see what happens? You can always go back to your old way of doing things if this doesn't work."

He agreed to my challenge and I left that day with a lot of hope. I couldn't wait to see him the next week and hear what happened. Can you guess what he said when I saw him seven days later?

Randy seemed to transform almost before my eyes. He told me that people nearly had double takes when he complimented them and encouraged them, letting them know he recognized and appreciated their hard work. He confided in me that it didn't feel easy or natural for him to do it, but there was no mistaking the universal reaction. People smiled; in fact, some absolutely beamed and worked all the harder at their jobs.

That was only the beginning of Randy learning how to use encouragement, and then coaching his people to guide and direct their progress. Next, he had to learn and practice how to talk about missed expectations, while still letting his people know he believed in them.

The skill of coaching includes giving people the facts, something like holding up a mirror for them to accurately see themselves. You let them know what is working and not working while at the same time encouraging them to improve.

When you don't know what to do to achieve a vital breakthrough, or you have tried everything else and it hasn't worked, why not resort to encouraging yourself and others? Learn to coach your people, helping them to obtain clarity and direction. Perhaps most of all, give them a reason to smile.

Hey, if it doesn't work, you can always go back to what you were doing.

Part Two

LEAD from the INSIDE OUT

What leaders do you most admire? What do you admire about them? Pick two of the leaders you most admire and answer the following questions:

- Why do you admire these leaders?
- What did they accomplish as leaders?
- Why do you think they chose to become leaders?
- What was their chief obstacle and eventual breakthrough?
- In what ways are you like them and how do you differ?

Each of the leaders you admire brought their own style to their leadership, and so do you. This means that perfecting your own leadership style is critical. If you want to become a sticky leader, you must learn to lead from the inside out. That's what makes sticky leaders so "sticky." And leading from the inside out occurs in three primary ways, each one building on the previous one.

First, sticky leaders practice self-leadership. If we can't lead ourselves, who would even consider following us? As we saw in Learning to Love Uphill, others are watching, using what they see to decide how to think and behave. Leading from the inside out means that what's inside us will leak out and become visible to others. Focusing on ourselves first, therefore, is crucial, and yet requires a high degree of self-awareness that's neither easy nor common.

Second, sticky leaders know they must lead the circumstances. Embracing your current reality—remembering the axiom that leaders can have no influence over something unless they have a relationship with it—means that inside-out leaders must become intimately familiar with what is and isn't happening around them, and then know what to do about it.

Finally, sticky leaders lead others by creating attractive change. People become curious when they see what you accomplished. They'll want to know how you did it. Many will come to you to learn and be influenced. Other forms of leadership appear manipulative when compared to sticky leadership, but having influence with others occurs naturally for the sticky leader.

PRACTICE SELF-LEADERSHIP

"Larry, you are a leader. You are here in the world to do great things. All these kids are looking up to you."

For me, the implied message I received from my father at a very early age amounted to this: "You'd better not screw up." There was a lot riding on being the eldest of what eventually would become nine kids in the Briggs family!

Today, I don't think my dad intended to communicate this message at all, but it's how I heard it. Over the years, as I really got to know my father, I realized he was an encourager by nature. Even so, although now I can see that I grew up in an atmosphere of intended encouragement and positive thinking, our family system didn't include the skills to talk about failure and missed expectations. Because we couldn't and didn't openly talk about what hadn't worked, we used non-verbal clues to express our disappointment. We filled in the silence with our own judgment of failures we recognized in ourselves.

This shame-filled environment produced in me a shame-based way of life. I worked hard to be perfect, but deep down, I knew I was flawed and failing those who most counted on me. I approached life by trying to look good on the outside in order to mask my deepest fear: If people really knew me, they would not like me or approve of me.

I wasn't popular in school and had few real friends, which

didn't help. The one or two close friends I had somehow seemed to like me regardless of my imperfections.

You can imagine how such a family history drove me. I was a mediocre student until I got into college, where I finally learned how to study. I got into subjects I liked and understood and so enjoyed a measure of real success. Maybe I was a late bloomer, I don't know. The fact is, I did quite well in college and my self-confidence grew—but the shame-based filter through which I experienced life remained. I continued to work hard to look good on the outside, while feeling deeply flawed on the inside. I expended my greatest effort to ensure that no one would ever know my deep, shameful secret.

I wasn't good enough—but I could fake it well.

COACHING CORNER

How do you experience leadership? What does it feel like to you? Why do you accept this leadership role anyway?

Your Past Helps to Shape Your Present

Does the way leaders think about themselves really matter? Do your thoughts impact your ability to lead under any and all circumstances? Does the motivation behind your leadership impact the approach you take to lead others? Does leadership feel like a burden to you? Does the fear of failing your leadership responsibilities weigh heavily on you? Do you fear looking bad in front of others? Or do you just not think about it at all?

If each of us examines our own stories of how we got to this place of leadership and how we somehow obtained the title, we can see how our personal history shapes how we wear it. Regardless of whether another bestowed the title upon us or if we reached out and claimed it for ourselves, our backstory propels us.

Your unique personal journey of how you got here and the way you understand your life experiences shapes how you think about yourself as leader. It is like your own internal programming that keeps running, whether you are aware of it or not. After many years of coaching executives and discovering their back stories and digging deeper into my own, I have come to the inescapable conclusion that how we lead is inevitably influenced by our history and the meaning we have made of it.

The saying, "No matter where you go, there you are," is often attributed to a Zen Buddhist ideal and quite possibly quoted from the cult movie Buckaroo Banzai. The point is, we can't escape ourselves. We bring all of who we are to the leadership process, and this includes our brilliance, our brokenness, our arrogance and our fears. To each leadership breakthrough we take on, we bring our compassion, faith, confidence (or lack thereof), as well as the many layers of meaning behind the stories we believe about ourselves. It is all either baggage or blessings, depending on how it works out in the moment. For this reason, sticky leadership is an inside out process.

Think of the leadership activity as a target. Each of us lies at the center of that target; we are the bullseye. And so, quite rightly, this is where both our focus and the source of our particular approach to leadership must begin.

Because we as leaders make things happen that otherwise would never take place, we work from the center of "reality," which underscores an important leadership point: Everyone has their own perception of what is happening around them at any point in time. You can think of each of us as touching the circumstances and each of us as having our own experience of those circumstances.

Most of us probably have heard the old Sufi Muslim story of the six blind men touching an elephant. Because their dead eyes wouldn't allow the men to see the entire beast at once, they could relate only to the part of the elephant they touched. Therefore the one with his hands on the trunk described the animal as a big, flexible hose. The one touching the side of the elephant strongly disagreed, insisting the creature was like a big wall covered with a tough hide. The man touching the ear thought the beast had huge leaves. The man touching the leg described the animal as something like the trunk of a thick tree. Finally, the one holding the tail proclaimed them all wrong; how could they fail to grasp that this creature was something like a rope?

We gain access to a very powerful leadership perspective by remembering that our own unique life experience is based on the way we perceive and relate to the circumstances that we "touch" at any moment. Couple this with the historical perspective of our own life story and the way in which past circumstances reminiscent of the current one turned out for us, and you can see the challenge that each of us faces when we choose to change the status quo.

One of my greatest breakthroughs in leadership and management occurred when I recognized two connected but seemingly opposite truths. First, people are like me in the way they experience reality, that is, from their own perspective. And second, because each of us is unique, with different life experiences, none of us experiences things in exactly the same way.

This level of complexity initially became a huge obstacle for me, because if I embraced it fully, I realized I would have to admit how very little I knew about how to proceed. After all, my views and thinking might or might not seem meaningful to others, due to our inherent differences. So if leadership is about influence, then how could I go about influencing others in a way that we all could begin to gain leverage over our circumstances, given our very different views, feelings, and expectations?

This challenge explains why leadership must begin with me, and only then extend to my perception of the current reality around me. I must grapple with myself before I can begin to think about others.

If I'm unusually fearful in a given situation, for example, I should try to apprehend those thoughts and process them first in order to obtain what I call leadership leverage, before attempting to ply any skill or authority to lead others. I've seen leaders jump to conclusions and make decisions for others that, in fact, were highly skewed by their own peculiar thinking and painful emotions. Those decisions often turned out badly.

We can't automatically assume that everyone sees things as we do, nor can we assume that they will react to circumstances as we would, which poses quite the dilemma for any leader. Concern over how to influence both the circumstances and others, in real time, can feel overwhelming, particularly for a new leader confronted both by unfavorable circumstances and by discouraged individuals.

Sticky leaders know that by beginning with themselves, they simplify any situation. And by focusing on the best way to personally influence those circumstances, they can demonstrate leadership in a way that builds confidence and trust.

Think of it as something like the trip instructions given by flight attendants. They tell us how oxygen masks will drop down automatically in an emergency, which we should affix to ourselves before attempting to help others. They don't mean to encourage selfishness; they simply know we can't help anyone if we pass out. To take care of others, we first have to take care of ourselves. Leaders create an unnecessary burden for their followers when they fail to attend first to self-leadership.

It All Begins with Me

What frustrates you most about the way you handle unwanted circumstances? Do you have a habit of answering your own questions before others have a chance to say anything? If you do, you should know that this does not produce sticky leadership.

Maybe you take action emotionally and intuitively, something that comes back to haunt you because you tend to overlook details that later bite. This habit doesn't build faith in your leadership capacity!

Or maybe you too easily give in to those who challenge your thinking, and later regret that you didn't remain firm in your convictions. This doesn't strengthen your credibility as a leader, either.

Or perhaps you wish you could think faster on your feet. Do you fear that because you rarely have a quick response, others judge you unfairly?

However you answered the questions, relax.

Each of us, if we are truly honest, must admit that we struggle with one or more of these chronic self-leadership challenges. If you couldn't come up with an answer to my questions, know that we all sometimes live in denial of our own unhelpful leadership behaviors. We try to survive by avoiding self-scrutiny. If that describes you, then this chapter may hold the key to your greatest personal leadership breakthrough. And if these ideas don't yet resonate with you, hang in there. I believe they will shortly.

For the rest of us—those who have identified that one thing that annoys us—can we agree that a few others may pop to the surface once we get the big one handled? None of us is perfect and we all can see gaps in our abilities when compared to our self-leadership ideal.

In my years of coaching executives, I've seen a very different pattern create great success. Transparent and humble leaders who recognize their flaws and openly work on them earn the admiration and even love of those around them. Tackling our self-leadership issues makes us stronger and gives us greater influence, rather than showing a sign of weakness. Because leadership is influence, self-leadership is the shortest pathway to developing sticky leadership.

It Matters More than You Think

I see some deep truth in what my father said to me so many years ago. He rightly noted, "Others are watching you." Once you declare your leadership, you get held to a higher standard. "But that's not fair!" someone objects. They may be right. But it's the truth.

As leaders, we use our influence to engage others in the Uphill work of changing current reality into something better. Only leaders perform this function, and even those who don't see themselves as leaders fulfill this role when they help others to Learn to Love Uphill. Accomplishing anything truly significant in this world is bigger than any one of us and takes more than what we can do by ourselves. Therefore, a leader must use the power of influence to bring enough leadership energy to bear on the circumstances, through other people, to change the course of events. As we do this, people are watching, and watching closely.

Why are they watching? They want to know, for one thing, if we really believe what we say. They check to see if our actions align with our words. Since my best leadership efforts don't always produce the desired effect, that can make for tough sledding. Why should I, an imperfect person deeply committed to positive change, be judged by a higher standard than others?

We all cope with this paradox differently. Some react by living out the phrase, "Do what I say, not what I do." But this strategy seldom works, and never works well. The world hates hypocrisy, especially in leaders. This one fact dissuades many from stepping into the leadership ranks, a sad thing because this world needs effective leaders.

Leading from the inside out, beginning with self, does not mean we have to be perfect, nor does it allow us to become hypocrites. It requires only that we be real.

Sticky Leaders Practice Vulnerability

Want to know something I find scary? Others can easily see me for who I am, rather than the person I want them to see. Observers can see me with more clarity than I can see myself. The harder I work to be someone I'm not, the more obvious it becomes to anyone watching.

Because inauthenticity feels deeply unattractive, it fails to create stickiness. If we have made positive leadership influence our goal, then we must carefully consider how others perceive us as we work on Loving Uphill. Sticky leadership is more caught than taught.

Can you remember any lectures from your childhood? I can, and I hated them. But it's not that the information in those lectures was wrong; in fact, I hated getting lectured because often the message landed pretty close to home. No, what I hated most about those lectures was the delivery. The parent was right and I was wrong. They were smart and I was foolish. I could grasp the point of the lecture if I chose to, but I could never get over the distasteful sense that I was clearly a subordinate. I hated that.

Sticky leadership, leading from the inside out, aims at creating a team of peers rather than using a hierarchical approach to accomplishing the work of Loving Uphill. A top-down style is a managerial approach to getting the uphill work done, and by definition that isn't leadership.

Vulnerability is a powerful leadership tool because it puts squarely on the table the reality that we all bring our personal history with us. In the Uphill work, we each run into our limitations as well as our strengths. Leading from the inside out prompts us to ask the question, "How can I use what limits me, in addition to what I clearly bring as strengths, to positively impact the status quo?"

Does this seem like an odd approach to self-leadership?

If so, consider a popular speaker who recently put herself, bravely, at the center of her own study on vulnerability. I'm speaking of Brené Brown, research professor and scholar who for more than a decade has studied leadership subjects such as courage, worthiness, shame and vulnerability. Her books focus on authentic leadership and wholeheartedness in families, schools and organizations. She has one of the most viewed TED talks ever, titled "The Power of Vulnerability." I highly recommend it.[6] In her YouTube talk, she models transparency and vulnerability—and judging by her enormous popularity (millions of views), you can see how many of us resonate with her message.

For self-aware leaders, Brené Brown provides a powerful example of self-leadership in action. We should never expect others to do anything they don't see us doing. Real leadership spreads by honest expressions of courage and truth telling. This kind of leadership cuts through the stinking thinking that gets in the way of the messages we want to send to influence others. But effective leadership has to begin with ourselves, so people see us as real people choosing to lead in the Uphill work by facing squarely the circumstances that confront us.

We don't just decide one day to become vulnerable and transparent, and then automatically make it so. Vulnerability and transparency come as a result of conscious effort, applied through self-leadership. They develop incrementally, over time. Consider some steps you can take to develop your own self-leadership as you Learn to Love Uphill.

1. **Don't expect others to do something you refuse to model yourself.**

   This step alone will immediately humble you—a fine

---

6 Brené Brown: "The power of vulnerability," filmed June 2010 at TEDxHouston

starting point for becoming more transparent and vulnerable.

2. **Identify where you already feel confident and comfortable about yourself.**

   Each of us has leadership areas where we can candidly speak of our difficult experience and the journey we have taken to get where we are. For me, this was public speaking. I started out as fearful, avoidant, and not very good at addressing groups. Today, I actually enjoy speaking in front of large audiences. When I began this uphill journey as a shy introvert so many years ago, I never would have guessed such a thing could happen.

   Find ways to describe how you achieved your competency and the confidence you now have. Reflect on how, at the beginning, you weren't very good, and yet you arrived where you are. Today you may even view yourself as having mastery in this area. This recognition should bring hope, to both you and others, that you can tackle other patterns of behavior and thinking that you want to change. You can make your desired change, even though it won't necessarily be easy or automatic. Knowing you have done it in one area makes it seem quite possible in some new area.

3. **Make a list of what you did, and the hurdles you overcame, to reach your current level of competency.**

   Notice the Uphill journey you took. You may not find it easy to reach back in time, but keep at it; this exercise yields powerful results. Remember the emotions and thoughts you had before you embarked on your Uphill journey to become as skilled as you now are. Those old thoughts and emotions probably mirror the ones you now have as you consider this newly targeted issue.

4. Clearly identify the self-leadership obstacle or constraint you want to convert to a breakthrough.

What is the constraint? What does it represent, and why is it important for you to eliminate it or transform it? What difference will this make in your self-leadership? Write out your thoughts in detail.

5. Recognize and own the relationship you have with this constraint.

You have a relationship with this issue, whether you recognize it or not. Maybe you avoid the relationship, but it's a relationship nonetheless. Remember that at the heart of leadership lies this fundamental truth: "Leaders can have no influence over something unless they have a relationship with it." In other words, leaders can change a thing only by getting in relationship with that thing. This is why many addicts can't change until they hit rock bottom. Until everything falls apart, they are not in relationship with their addiction. They pretend it doesn't exist. So a key principle of leadership is developing the ability to get in relationship with anything we want to influence. This is why beginning with self-leadership is so crucial. The effort is real, close to home, and gives us a place to practice this skill in a way that can have huge impact on all aspects of our leadership.

> **"Leaders can have no influence over something unless they have a relationship with it."**
>
> *–Larry Briggs*

So get in touch with the relationship you already have with this behavior or thinking that you want to change. Recognize how you feel about your desire to change—fearful, frustrated, lacking confidence, unskillful, avoidant, or whatever words describe why you haven't yet mastered this issue. And then clearly define your vision for the ideal. What do you want the change to make possible? You can generally get a good idea here by thinking about the opposite of what exists today. Perhaps you want to feel confident, skillful, capable, powerful, or maybe even experience some joy in the process. Take time to write down and envision what it would be like for you to thoroughly own this new capability.

6. **Determine with whom you will share your commitment to this new process of change.**

This final step activates everything else. Pick someone who will encourage you when you need it and hold you accountable when you want to give up. Meet with this person and candidly let him or her know you want help in this process. Practice talking about the change you haven't yet made, but are Learning to Love Uphill in the quest to make it real. After you have this conversation, recognize that when you open up about your commitment to this kind of personal change, you will naturally model vulnerability and self-leadership. It really is as simple (and as hard) as that.

Once you find the courage to actually do this, I promise that it gets easier. Look to others who have done this (or are doing it) for inspiration and recognize that you have joined the ranks of other leaders who have chosen to transparently Learn to Love Uphill. This will encourage others, because although it doesn't always look pretty, they see that genuine leaders won't give up on the process. So burn the boats and keep going. It gets easier in time.

Self-Talk and Self-Leadership

How do you talk to yourself? Don't deny it, we all do it. Probably not out loud very often, but we talk to ourselves all the time. It's called self-talk.

You already know how easy it is to talk yourself into something you really want to do, and you know how to talk yourself out of it later, just as easily. We use the term "buyer's remorse" to describe such a flip-flop in the process of purchasing some expensive item. All of us can talk ourselves into and out of many things, and we may not even notice when we do so.

Becoming aware of how we talk to ourselves, and increasing our mindfulness of what we say to ourselves, lies at the heart of good self-leadership. It marks the beginning of the Uphill journey to positive self-awareness.

I've noticed a pattern among those I coach. We tend to talk to ourselves in ways that closely echo how we speak to others. Show me a man who speaks harshly to others, and I will show you someone even harsher on himself. On the other hand, you may tell yourself some pretty nasty things that you would never think of saying, out loud, to someone else. Do you notice that you can be harder on yourself than you are on others? Is this because you don't trust yourself, or don't like yourself, or feel most resistant to your own leadership influence?

Over time, sticky leaders develop the important skill of intentionally talking to themselves in helpful ways. They closely monitor what they say to themselves as they work on the uphill part of their breakthrough. You can start right now by consciously noting what you say to yourself, particularly when things become difficult. Does your self-talk help or hurt your ability to do what you've promised yourself or others? The more you become aware of this internal conversation, the larger your leadership capacity will grow.

The Most Important Self-leadership Question

The single most important self-leadership question is this:

To what are you committed?

I learned about commitment years ago when I invested deeply in a self-awareness training seminar, led by one of the top authorities of the time. It seemed I had reached a pinnacle in my career in the software industry, but I found myself unfulfilled and cranky. My marriage felt mediocre, my earnings had plateaued, my two young sons got little of my time, and while companies looking for CEO candidates had begun to recruit me, I didn't feel motivated to pursue their offers, even though they appeared to imply increases in earnings, prestige, and career development.

What was wrong with me? I couldn't figure it out and my befuddlement drove me into counseling, self-development programs and extended times of prayer and meditation. For a while, all these efforts seemed fruitless. I struggled for months, and those close to me could see it. I felt like a starving man seated at a table overflowing with delicacies of all kinds, but who had no appetite for anything set before him. Nothing seemed to fill me up or satisfy my cravings. I know it sounds crazy. I felt as though I might be losing my mind.

Then I learned about the role and power of commitment—and things suddenly began to make sense. Today I know that commitment lies at the heart of leadership. Let me explain it in a way that I hope you might benefit from my struggles.

As a leader, all you have to work with is what people will commit to.

If you leave with only one idea from this book, take this one, apply it and use it. Commitment lies at the heart of leadership. Study commitment, see it in action in your own life, and then help others recognize its power. This single concept, when deeply known and put in action, will transform your leadership capacity.

And, of course, commitment is best studied in and for yourself.

I've heard people compare commitment to a promise. No doubt you have heard someone say, "They made a commitment to do that," or, "He committed to following through on this." But a commitment differs from a promise and it certainly is not the same thing as an agreement. One can make an agreement and have little or no commitment to honoring that agreement. This is important to recognize, because this very issue causes many of the leadership breakdowns we all see. We must come to understand commitment and the significant role it plays in our life and how it anchors our happiness and fulfillment.

A good way to begin understanding commitment and how it works is to think about a battery. What does a battery do? It provides energy, a power source **Commitment is like a battery for our lives.** for a machine, instrument, or tool. Our cars use batteries to get started. Batteries power flashlights. Space vehicles have batteries, often recharged by solar panels, that store energy for later use, enabling them to operate untended for many years. Without the invention of the battery, many devices we take for granted would not be possible, thus eliminating many of the conveniences we so love.

Commitment is like a battery for our lives.

Think of commitment as the energy source for what animates your life. Remember the statement at the heart of this chapter: As a leader, all you have to work with is what people will commit to. Whatever we commit to is the thing that gets us going and sustains us. When you set off on an Uphill journey, what will sustain you, particularly when things get difficult? It's your commitment. Understanding the nature and depth of your commitment will help you to know what you can count on when things get difficult.

Before I give you an example, let's recognize that all of us have a mountain of commitments, ranked in order from most to least important. We have commitments to health, to happiness, to relationships, to our faith practices, to our careers, and so on. While we may share some of these commitments in common, the depth of our commitment (how much stored energy is available for us to use) and the relative rank of that commitment can vary. One man may be more committed to his health than another, particularly when challenged by a competing commitment of enjoyment. If I rank my commitment to enjoyment above my health, I could find myself consuming tasty foods and sugary drinks without regard for my health, which could result in obvious changes in my weight and fitness.

Each of us has the freedom to choose our own particular set of commitments. And despite what anyone may say to us or about us, our actions will line up with our true commitments (as opposed to what we think our commitments ought to be).

Many of us struggle with how our actions sometimes war against what our minds tell us is right. We may know beyond a shadow of a doubt that some tempting habit or food harms us, but still find ourselves repeatedly caving in to that temptation. At that point, our true commitment becomes clear. We will always spend our time, energy, and money on that to which we are truly committed, as opposed to what we say we want or think we should be doing.

I made this discovery many years ago during my struggle to make sense of my life. Although recruiters regularly talked to me about taking top jobs in other software companies, positions that likely would have increased my earnings and advanced my career, I didn't feel motivated to pursue any of them. And I wondered, What is going on?

Once the role of commitment began to come clear to me, I decided to list all of the things to which I thought I was committed. The list looked something like this:

Family *(I had two small sons at the time)*
Marriage
Career
Health
Giving Back to Others
Spiritual Faith
Fun
Learning
Creating things of Value
Travel

The list continued beyond those items as I tried to identify everything I could think of that felt important to me. I wanted to see, in black and white, my authentic commitments, those things into which I would willingly invest time, money, and effort.

Once I completed my list, I set out to rank each item, asking myself with as much honesty as I could muster, "Is this more important than that?" I wanted to know what things really had my strongest commitment. I then created a simple, two-column table that looked something like this:

Rank Ordered Commitments *(most important to least)*	The Degree to Which I Am Actually Investing Myself in This Commitment

By performing this exercise, I made a revealing discovery that underscored my long-time dilemma. I found, to my surprise and dismay, that my stated commitments bore little resemblance to how I actually spent most of my time, money, and efforts.

What did this revelation mean? Did it mean that I had erred in my ordering of personal commitments, or did it mean that my actual commitments in fact showed up in the second column? I had placed career as my top commitment; but then why hadn't I jumped at all those new job opportunities that would seem to have better satisfied that commitment?

Something here didn't add up. I had to figure it out.

At the same time, my wife and I had begun some marriage counseling. I believed that our marital struggles, if left unchecked, could take us in a very bad direction. While neither of us had mentioned divorce, we both felt unhappy and wanted to understand why.

In the conversation that ensued, I heard my wife talk about her father, a dairyman and a very hard worker. I heard her say that her dad would go out of his way for others, including his cousins and siblings, often at the expense of his own family. She expressed both sadness and anger at this experience, and then revealed her greatest fear: She had married someone like her father, who would sacrifice his family to other commitments.

That single revelation gave deep meaning to my table exercise about commitment. I recognized that, in fact, I had a strong commitment to my family and my marriage, but that I had not honored that commitment. Instead, I had sacrificed it for career and material rewards. A profoundly painful realization! At that moment, I decided that if I had accurately ranked my commitments—and I believed I had— then I needed to live an honest life by doing a better job of lining up my true commitments with my actions, especially in my investment of time, effort, and money. That realization led eventually to a key insight about self-leadership. Sticky leaders embrace the following truth:

Learning to Love Uphill in my own life includes an honest accounting of my true commitments, then aligning my actions with my most important commitment areas.

I quickly learned that aligning my actions with my true commitments was no easy task. I had built bad habits through years of repeated behaviors. I also began to recognize that I had a "pleaser" mentality and would often make unwise agreements and put energy into activities I felt others wanted from me, rather than acting from my own key commitment areas.

As hard as it was, and as long as it took me to live a more honest life in regard to my key commitments, I reaped a great reward in the form of greater satisfaction and joy. I found the root of self-leadership in this process of alignment. I recognized that I had not jumped at the offered job opportunities because I had some level of awareness that taking any of those jobs would mean a move, which would not honor my commitment to my family. All of us loved where we lived, in Oregon.

I also recognized that I have workaholic tendencies, possibly just like my wife's father. Putting myself into a job that would deepen those behaviors would injure my health, my family, and ultimately my true happiness. So how could that be a good decision?

Sticky leaders recognize that self-leadership requires honesty, especially in aligning our actions with our true commitments. Acting on our actual commitments strengthens the commitment. It gives us more battery power when things get difficult, releasing energy stored within the commitment.

A Heart for Leadership

Sticky Leaders practice the rare but crucial discipline of getting to know their hearts. Even more important, perhaps, they discover the purpose of their hearts.

"Larry," you might respond, "we all know what the heart is for. It pumps blood throughout the body." From a physiological perspective, you would be right. But what else is the heart for?

Throughout history, cultures worldwide have placed special importance on the heart. Most ancient peoples knew that it pumped blood throughout the body, but they also attributed to it a much larger role. The Bible says, for example, "Above all else, guard your heart, for it is the wellspring of life" (Proverbs 4:23, NIV). In the Bible's very last chapter, we hear the Spirit of God say, "I am he who searches mind and heart, and I will give to each of you according to your works" (Revelation 2:23, ESV). Even today, probably you have heard someone say about a co-worker whose performance fell well below expectations, "Obviously, his heart just wasn't in it."

Our "hearts" play an important role in leadership, and the first job of a sticky leader is to get to know their own heart and what their heart is for.

COACHING CORNER

Do you have a heart for leadership?
If so, for what does your heart beat most strongly?

You can't really prioritize a list of your key commitments without first considering your heart. We all can claim a deep commitment to something noble—let's say, giving back to the community—and then later admit that our heart really wasn't in it. Or we can say we are committed to something, and even act in some small way to back up that commitment; but if our heart really isn't in it, our energy at some point will begin to flag. Our efforts will become mechanical, as if we're just going through the motions. We've all seen it happen.

I've met leaders who have trained and disciplined themselves so thoroughly that they have distanced themselves from the true desires of their hearts, to such a degree that they don't even know their hearts any longer. It's sad. But it's also bad news for their leadership. Leaders who don't even know their own hearts find it very difficult to make their leadership sticky. People feel attracted to genuine passion, and heartless leadership generates very little of it.

Untrained and unsupervised, our hearts can grow selfish, corrupt, fearful, and even dangerous. My brother, a doctor of natural medicine, treats patients suffering from various diseases that he firmly believes began in their minds and hearts. Our hearts can grow unhealthy, both physically and spiritually. If we don't know our hearts and learn how to take care of them, we will never make the Uphill journey to becoming a true sticky leader.

So then—how well do you know your heart?

I've worked with hundreds of highly successful entrepreneurs and I've seen how highly driven leaders can override their deepest desires for so long that they completely lose touch with their hearts. They become totally driven by the head rather than the heart. And their people usually suffer for it.

To effectively work with our people, we have to understand ourselves well enough to recognize attributes, behaviors and desires in others that remind us of our own. But if we don't recognize these things in ourselves, then how can we see them in others? Inside out leadership emphasizes the importance of getting to know your heart.

Sustainable Leadership—A Matter of the Heart

The leaders who endure are usually the ones most connected to their own hearts. When we talk about the heart, we find something of depth that just doesn't show up when we talk about the head. We can all sense a leader who spends all of his time in his head, without ever accessing his heart. We may see his actions as "logical," but not emotionally grounded. Those who live out of their head and heart tend to last longer and enjoy life more.

Being heart-lead takes into account things that, at first blush, may seem subtle, but in the end, make all the difference. Leaders with heart seldom have trouble finding people who will follow. For me, that leader was John Gorman, the first president and co-founder of Timberline Software. I watched him willingly subordinate himself to others, and not just because of his intelligence. He did this authentically because it resonated with his very large heart. And his people happily followed his lead. Today, many years after his retirement, those of us who worked for him so many years ago still speak glowingly of him. I tend to think his heart colored his decisions and how he treated each of us. And therefore he left a universal impression on all of us.

Another heart-led leader, author and speaker Bob Goff, has been quoted as saying, "The battle for our hearts is fought on the pages of our calendar."[7] Bob is a successful businessman and attorney, as well as a New York Times best-selling author and speaker. His book, *Love Does*, is a sort of memoir that chronicles the way he thinks and acts. In it, he tells stories that seem almost beyond belief. One day, for example, he asked his kids what they would ask world leaders if they had five minutes with them. The Goff children sent invitations to many world leaders, asking them to come to their house for a sleepover. In response, the Goff family got invited to visit the royal palaces of twenty-nine global leaders. Goff took his kids out of school and visited every one of them. As a result of the world tour and his observation of both human need and terrible injustice, Bob started Restore International in 2003 to "find daring, productive and effective ways to fight the injustices committed against children." In addition to being a smart founder of a legal firm specializing in construction defect litigation, Bob is making a difference globally as a leader by taking action on the things that both make sense and resonate with his heart.

Aligning your heart with your head makes for longevity of leadership. So what about your own heart? What issues cause you the most struggles? Some decisions feel right on the surface and lend themselves to logical defense. But ultimately, you have an uneasy feeling about them, even though you can't immediately identify the problem. Your heart tells you

---

7   Bob Goff: *Love Does.*

that something is wrong somewhere. And so you override a decision that seems logically right.

The truth is, the mind alone can lead us down some very dark alleys. The architects of "the Final Solution" in Nazi Germany used their very sharp brains to construct extremely well designed death camps in Auschwitz, in Treblinka, in Bergen-Belsen, and elsewhere. At least six million Jews went to their deaths as directed by very smart, very refined, very well educated men whose hearts had shriveled. Head without heart, logic without compassion, can create "results" that leaves scars for generations. Had "good hearts" prevailed in Germany, history may well have unfolded very differently.

The situation is little better, of course, if we opt for all heart and no head. I've seen entrepreneurs delay in letting employees go during a downturn, only to go out of business— and all because they didn't take the appropriate financial actions that their intellect insisted they had to take. *The point here is not either/or, but both/and. Choosing to be an inside out, sticky leader means being both smart and having a heart.* The both/and leads to sustainability.

Think of the head and heart connection as something like the checks and balances system designed by our Founding Fathers when they worked hard to create a country different from any other. These brilliant men recognized that brilliance, left unchecked, could lead to things like kings treating colonists with contempt. So they developed a system of government in which three independent branches would share power in multiple ways, making it very difficult for any one of those branches to start acting like King George. The judicial branch, the executive branch, and the legislative branch would all have to work together to protect the country and move it forward. And what happens when they fail to do so effectively? Gridlock. Decline. Rancor. They all need to work together.

The heart can be wrong or misguided, just as the head can be wrong and misguided. Our hearts may yearn for ultimate power, wealth, and selfish pleasures, and so require the checks and balances supplied by the head. In this way, we keep on track and moving forward. The ultimate self-leadership practice is to become acutely aware of both head and heart, taking note of when they align and when they don't.

Getting our hearts aligned with our heads may cause us to re-examine the values by which we guide our businesses, and perhaps consider a few changes intended to make things better, healthier, more consistent, and more sustainable. Understanding our hearts and those of others will help us to engage in deep, genuine, and heartfelt conversations that can show us new ways to improve service, innovation, and profitability. And what sticky leader wouldn't want that?

It Only Makes Sense

It all boils down to this: If we can't lead ourselves, then what makes us think we can change our circumstances for the better? Why would we think we could positively influence others? It only makes sense to take on the most difficult constraint we face if we want to create a breakthrough—and for many of us, that most difficult constraint is learning how to lead ourselves.

It takes humility to embrace our incompleteness, our brokenness, and our fallibility, and sticky leaders do so with eyes wide open. They embrace the reality of their circumstances and they recognize their own inability to be perfect. They accept the inherent limitations that all of us have. If we as leaders can't love ourselves enough to see ourselves for who we really are, warts and all, then we won't have any influence over ourselves.

For that reason, sticky leaders know that "it all begins with me."

LEAD the CIRCUMSTANCES

Leaders who make good things happen are always in demand. How many volatile situations in our world need the attention of sticky leaders?

Think of sticky leadership as the application of a unique type of applied energy that starts a cascading process that eventually leads to radical change. This process involves creating improvements that encourage others to give their very best, enabling sticky leaders to attract and keep key personnel.

Imagine the right people catching your leadership vision, and then watching as your efforts to do the right thing spread like a virus to others. Your vision soon crescendos into a movement that positively impacts some crucial part of your world.

And so everyone wins.

Does that sound out of reach for you? It isn't. I invite you to think bigger. History is rich with examples of dynamic movements started by just one person armed with a vision, a sticky leader willing to take action to make something good happen.

Circumstances First

We typically think of a leader having influence over people, but what if leaders also have influence over life's circumstances? I think of Dr. Martin Luther King. He looked at the circumstances of his world, and while he completely recognized that people had created the way things were, he spoke to the circumstances. He focused on people second, not first. He saw his mission as a leader to change the way things were—the reality then in existence—and so he spoke to the circumstances of his society. You remember his words:

> *I have a dream that one day on the red hills of Georgia the sons of former slaves and the sons of former slave-owners will be able to sit down together at a table of brotherhood.*
> — Martin Luther King, Jr.

When we focus on the situation before concentrating on the people, we bring a powerful dynamic to our leadership. Our ability to depersonalize a situation helps us to better recognize its complex nature. To change the current reality, we must develop the ability to envision something better than what we see currently. Sticky leaders know how to speak to the circumstances with a view toward influencing them for the better.

All of us feel a natural attraction to sticky leadership wherever it shows up. Each of us is looking for someone to step out, inspire us, and bring forward some compelling vision that resonates with our hearts. We want such leaders to call us to join them in a purpose and vision greater than ourselves—we want to become partners in changing current reality to make a better life for all. We feel drawn to the new set of circumstances, captivated by a vision we can identify with, and energized by the idea of joining others in bringing an exciting new future into existence.

Leadership is fundamentally about change, an alteration from the way things are to some new and better way they could be. That includes change in the circumstances around us and change in the way we live, think, and enjoy our lives. Such change helps us to become positive contributors to a better world.

The Meaning in Circumstances

In my years of working closely with people of all types at very risky and vulnerable times, I've received a glimpse into basic human nature. I find that when we feel honest, healthy, and loved, we want nothing more than to give back to others. When we feel blessed, joyful, inspired, and even challenged, the best version of ourselves surfaces and we get in touch with a purpose in life far bigger than our own petty concerns. We start envisioning a future better than the present.

In our times of greatest inspiration, we often gain true spiritual insight as we get a glimpse into the true desires of our hearts, deep longings that transcend selfishness and aim at alleviating the suffering of those in need or in discomfort. In short, we want to change the way things are.

Leadership focused on changing difficult circumstances isn't easy, but it is worth it.

COACHING CORNER

What do you focus on when there is an uphill challenge?

I'm reminded of a "Ryan," a CEO whose sixteen-year-old daughter died at the hands of a drunk driver. The tragedy occurred only months after he engaged me to help him with his manufacturing company. I was probably one of the few men in Ryan's life with whom he could fully let down and reveal the intense pain he felt over his massive loss. I remember attending the funeral and how that shared experience deepened our relationship on both a personal and a business level.

Ryan had hired me to help him find ways to have more fun and become more effective in bringing his business vision into reality. The deep personal loss caused by the death of his only daughter helped bring a measure of transparent reality into our business conversations. Our talks quickly moved to looking for meaning beyond the requirements of a profitable business. Ryan recognized his desire to change the way things were and set out to do something to make that change happen.

Profoundly painful life experiences sometimes bring a clarity we wouldn't otherwise have, especially in how we lead our lives and direct our careers. As odd as it sounds to look for blessing in such times of deep darkness, I believe the question is worth asking: "Why should I have to deal with such difficult circumstances? Why me?"

Maybe the better question to ask is, why not me?

The Bible says the rain falls on the just and unjust alike. No one seems to have immunity from senseless tragedy or an exemption from deep disappointment. Things happen in our lives and we must figure out how to deal with the aftermath. Tragic events like Ryan's will make us either bitter or better. As easy it is for us to shake our fist at God and ask "why me?" maybe a better approach is to allow the tragedy to bring us greater clarity about our life purpose as a leader. Maybe the better question is really, "What good can come from this heartbreak?"

Sticky leaders know that the way things ultimately go has much to do with how we embrace the current reality of our circumstances. Our willingness to use pain and discomfort can help us to become better leaders with higher aspirations beyond personal rewards and success.

I had the privilege of coaching Ryan for several years, and at some point, one of his assembly line workers got caught dealing drugs. The young man ended up serving a year in jail.

Just before this individual got released, I happened to learn, almost by accident, that Ryan had visited his former employee in prison every week, bringing him fresh reading material and maintaining a personal connection throughout the man's time behind bars. Furthermore, when the young man got out of prison, Ryan gave him back his old job.

Do you think this man's life changed as a result of what Ryan did for him? Upon his return to freedom and resuming his old job, he certainly appeared to be a changed man. He let very few know what his boss had done for him, but as a transformed, model employee, he quickly became a leader in his own right.

Was there any connection between Ryan's tragic loss of a beloved daughter and the way he later extended himself to an employee who had failed so publicly? I can only speculate about a link, but it seems highly likely to me.

As an observer, I can tell you that Ryan's entire business culture seems to have significantly improved in the aftermath of both events. Today the company thrives in its industry, with an intensely loyal workforce. Ryan's son is in the process of taking over the leadership of the business.

As leaders, we have a choice about finding meaning in our circumstances. We find leadership leverage over our current reality, in part, by bringing meaning to the experience, which requires intimacy with the circumstances. Sticky leaders develop the ability to embrace what's occurring around them without giving up on the vision and the importance of changing things for the better.

Get into Relationship with the Circumstances

If leaders make things happen that otherwise would not have occurred, what responsibility do you have over your current circumstances?

Remember the obstacle you identified in Part One, Learning to Love Uphill? Take a closer look at it. This obstacle will serve up two clues you can use to find leverage.

1. What is happening now that you believe needs to change?

2. Describe your vision of the ideal. What do you want the circumstances to become?

While it may seem daunting to note the big gap between what is and what could be, sticky leaders all know this:

No gap, no leadership.

How do you use your energy in the gap to change what's happening now to what you believe needs to happen in the future? That's leadership. The more clarity you have about the gap, the more skillfully you can exercise an influence over the current reality. Max DePree understood this well many years ago:

> *The first responsibility of a leader is to define reality. The last is to say thank you. In between the two, the leader must become a servant and a debtor.*
>
> Max DePree, *Leadership Is an Art*

Some leadership thinking jumps right to what we need to do with people, but the sticky leadership model starts with self-leadership. It's an inside out approach, which requires that we first have an influence over ourselves. Who will respect a leader who can't be himself what he asks of others? We have no choice but to tackle self-leadership, because our integrity is at stake.

This second section of the book emphasizes that we won't have any credibility as leaders without exerting some influence over the circumstance. The whole world is looking for leaders who can change the status quo for the better. So how do you gain an influence over the circumstances? You get in relationship with the circumstances, which means you must become intimately familiar with them.

We all have experienced or heard stories about leaders who come in with guns blazing and immediately begin to bark out orders for change. People have little respect for these kinds of leaders, because at some level, we all know they don't have an intimate relationship with what's really going on. They've made some assumptions about who, what, and how things are working, but they don't really know. They're not in it. They hover around, just outside the fray. We resent this because they haven't taken the time to really understand the situation, what people are thinking, what has been tried, and the reasons things remain as they are. In reality, things are nearly always more complex than they at first appear.

Your job as a sticky leader is to begin addressing the circumstances with personalized simplicity. Leaders who get intimate with their current reality know that:

1. There is a reason for the way things are.

2. Inertia is real and changing the status quo will take focused energy.

3. Being smart recognizes that a shared vision of an ideal future has a power all its own that can be used to pull the circumstances toward that better future.

4. Energy and resources are always limited and therefore require wise use.

5. Some of the limiting factors hide under the surface and don't reveal themselves until leaders apply energy to the key constraint. Only then will sufficient intimacy with the current reality make the situation clear.

6. Altering the circumstances is your first job as a leader. You must model what changing the circumstances requires and looks like. That means you must begin acting differently.

The Need for Simple Leverage

Some of the smartest people in history had some very profound things to say about simplicity.

"If you can't explain it to a six year old, you don't understand it yourself."
— Albert Einstein

"I would not give a fig for the simplicity this side of complexity, but I would give my life for the simplicity on the other side of complexity."
— Oliver Wendell Holmes, Jr.

The key to getting leverage over your circumstances is to make both leadership and your circumstances simple. Simplicity has tremendous power.

Unfortunately, in leadership it's easy to get confused. So remember that while leadership is about influence, management is about control. Therefore, consider a smart self-leadership question to ask: "In this circumstance, do we need leadership or management?" It's a simple question with profound ramifications.

Do you need to take control over things or have influence over them? Our first reaction may be to choose control; but influence often generates far better results.

In order to know whether you need to exercise leadership or management, you must simplify the problem, which requires you to become deeply familiar with it. Most of us, particularly when we judge a situation as unfriendly, unhappy, or unfavorable, want to move on to better thoughts and ideas. I can't tell you the number of times I've cautioned coaching clients to slow down and avoid moving into problem solving before they become completely intimate with the true nature of their obstacles. Such an extended time of exploration can feel painful or uncomfortable, or even like a big waste of time and energy, but it is critical. When we know something well, we can understand how best to exert influence over the various elements of our circumstances.

We don't always get good models of this type of leadership. Our government, for example, appears to think that throwing money at a problem can usually solve it. Don't make that mistake! When you exercise enough patience to decode the situation and divide it into its component parts, you will begin to see the real kinks in the hose. You can then identify the biggest one and start developing a strategy to create a breakthrough. To simplify a set of circumstances, break it down into its various parts and see how they all work together.

One of my clients designs and manufactures very high quality leather products that it sells online. Customers from around the world love the company's bags and take pictures of themselves with their beloved gear in all kinds of situations, including skydiving, car racing, fishing, camping, and at work.

The president and founder of the company is a creative genius. I met him when serving another client on site in Africa, and not long thereafter, he called me with a problem he needed to solve. The company had stopped growing and he worried that his management team wasn't working together properly to take the company to the next level. He wanted me to help him determine if he had the right people in the right positions. He also asked me to assist him in developing a shared vision that embraced that next business level he felt everyone wanted.

One thing became obvious after interviewing each of his team members and facilitating a weekend offsite retreat. The president got involved in every aspect of the business, bringing his wealth of new ideas and strong opinions about how things should be done wherever he went. Unfortunately, his passionate involvement felt so disruptive that at least one of his employees had begun to consider whether he should leave the company that he so deeply loved and helped to build. I found such intense and mixed feelings toward the president that morale was plummeting and a flurry of "kinks in the hose" threatened to overwhelm everyone. A downward spiral of lost business and employee turnover seemed imminent.

Developing a refined, shared vision seemed like the easy part. Everyone felt happy to contribute his or her ideas of what it might look like. The far harder job was to figure out a simple solution to the main problem, namely, that the president wanted to get involved in every part of the business, often disrupting manufacturing, shipments, marketing programs and the like. Creativity is great, but when expressed in every part of the business—particularly when people feel under the gun to get work done, customers served, and budgets met—it can become deeply frustrating and unwelcome. Not something the president wanted to hear! Hadn't creativity set up the company for success?

And yet they came up with a simple solution. They created a flat business model with an R & D lab at the very beginning of the process, with the rest of the firm's activities—including marketing, sales, order processing, manufacturing and shipping—each occurring at their natural stage in the process. That led to a happy customer at the end of the work chain. Everyone could understand this simple model for how the business worked. Creative ideas about products and how to get work done came up front and got thought out completely before any other activities and expenditures.

As you can imagine, the president found his playhouse in the R & D lab. Here he explores and tests his ideas about how the business makes product, sells it, and promotes it to customers. He can pull "advisors" from other parts of the company into the lab to provide input and to verify that the company could execute these ideas throughout the life cycle of the proposed product. The only requirement: Creativity and new, untested ideas had to remain in the R & D lab. What became "kits"—executable plans with instructions for implementation—could then be used to measure the success and financial prudence of the lab itself.

Simplifying the business, and the way everyone thought about the business and how work got done (including high creative work), began a process of streamlining that eventually helped the company to achieve its next level of achievement. It reached its vision.

For this company, getting beyond complexity to simplicity required embracing the truth about why things worked and why they didn't. None of it came easy. But they hit the jackpot, in both productivity and morale.

Mastering Current Reality

You will know when you have begun to gain mastery over your current reality—and it may come sooner than you expect. When you begin to think differently about the GAP between your inspired vision and the circumstances, you are on the right track. And when you begin to view your difficult circumstances as something useful, potent, and engaging, you will have taken the first step in leading in the circumstances.

To a sticky leader, there is no such thing as good news or bad news; there is only news. When the leader is in relationship with current reality, the circumstances represent potential fuel, inspiration, and catalytic energy to be leveraged. Such a leader then has the ability to exercise influence over events.

Remember, influence differs from control. You can have influence but still lack control. To a sticky leader, it feels a bit like surfing. Surfers don't control the wave, but they know how to ride it and use it to take them to where they want to go, while enjoying the ride along the way. Leading in the circumstances feels a lot like that: Exciting, powerful, useful, and often even fun.

I think of one of my early lessons in leading in the circumstances. A year after I became the top salesman for my software company, I got promoted to sales manager. All seemed right with the world as I began moving up the ranks. I looked forward to working with the director of sales and marketing and the other members of his team, all of whom I admired. They also had landed their leadership roles as a result of their solid field sales performance.

I flew into the office over the Thanksgiving holiday to prepare my sales budget for the next year and to get ready to begin my new position right after the New Year. But first thing Monday morning, the president called me into his office to deliver some shocking news. After much personal debate and with the counsel of the board of directors, he had fired the entire sales and marketing leadership staff. It had become painfully clear they could not produce the results they had been promising. I didn't know that company sales had taken a nosedive or that the sales and marketing leadership had failed to turn things around, even though for months they had confidently promised that things would improve.

Like any opportunist, I quickly volunteered to take over the entire leadership of sales and marketing. I offered to assume the role of my boss and his associates. I saw an opportunity and took it.

What was I thinking?

The days that followed were among the most difficult and stressful of my career. Even though I had led my first business turnaround in my mid-twenties, the magnitude of this challenge far exceeded anything I had ever done. I felt excited and terrified, all at the same time. I knew that all of us in the field shared the vision for our company dominating the market, but I also knew that if all twenty-eight sales people saw the changes at corporate in a negative light, they would leave for better opportunities elsewhere. And that would sink us as a company. Somehow, I needed to obtain everyone's trust in my leadership, without maligning our former leadership.

Over the next three days, I had long phone calls with each member of the field sales team. I used those conversations to learn how they were doing and then carefully told the story about how the beloved and admired previous leadership had been unable to turn the tide on declining sales. I shared my personal commitment to each sales person's success and the success of the company, while clearly illuminating the challenges we all faced in turning around the trend. I reinforced and endorsed the shared vision of market domination we all dreamed of for our accounting software products.

No one quit. Things remained difficult for the next few months as we all worked hard to turn things around. By sharing the commitment we all had for personal and team success, we locked arms and began to discuss the things that were not working, some of which the corporate office could address. Slowly the trend reversed, and we rebuilt the sales and marketing leadership team.

Despite those scary and difficult times, we managed to strengthen the field sales team even though we lost a few folks over the ensuing months. We also drove some product refinements that eventually led, a few years later, to fulfilling our vision of market domination. As a team, we mastered our current reality. And as a newbie leader, I got a taste for what it feels like to lead the circumstances and so lead a team into the winner's circle.

The Vision to Action Leadership Model (V2A)

What if leading people is just one way to use your leadership energy? When you use your energy to influence the circumstances, to change the way things are, you also are leading.

In the V2A model, once we decide to act as sticky leaders, we focus first on the current reality we want to change, based on our commitments. By knowing what we don't want, we can begin to imagine what we do want—what would seem inspiring and ideal. Without a vision of what can be possible, we have no way of gaining clarity about our key commitment area, and we lack the ability to enroll others in something that may inspire them as well.

Once we have a vision for the ideal, we can begin to share it with others whom we believe may want to join us in changing things for the better. This is the way leaders build a team to accomplish something big. All great visions are bigger than what any individual could accomplish on his or her own, and the people who join have common commitments expressed by the inspiring vision.

After we have assembled a team of people who share the vision, we can ask the important question about what we consider most important in the way we go about creating change. Understanding the heartbeat of the vision and what people most value will help to shape our approach. Honoring our values and those of others creates value and multiplies the resources and the energy available to us to achieve the breakthrough.

Setting goals together is an important way to measure progress toward the vision and provides us with the focus to work together on short-term objectives. Since we agree these objectives are meaningful to all of us, we hold each other accountable for the parts we choose to tackle.

Once we know the where and when of our journey toward the vision, we have to develop a strategy to fulfill it, which is nothing more than describing a way through difficulty to reach our goals.

After we have our strategy in place, we need to communicate it clearly, both inside and outside of our team. As we do so, we realize that keeping the vision in front of us and working together to move forward to reach each of our goal milestones will test both our resolve and the relationships within our leadership team. Only good communication can sustain coordinated, smart action. Sticky leadership is viral, and working together to practice self-leadership and effective ways to lead, given our circumstances, requires that we effectively and continually communicate.

Once we have a working strategy and are in constant

communication, sticky leaders create processes and routines to bring automation and repetition to how we use our energy to bring the vision into reality. If we can define the process for how our various kinds of energy combine to move current reality toward the vision (and our goal milestones), we also demonstrate that we have enough intimacy with the circumstances to influence them. Leaders who don't have a process reveal they don't really understand the circumstances sufficiently to know how to influence them.

Once effective processes get developed[7], we need to share them with everyone in the organization. Sticky leaders believe in training and learning together so that everyone can continually improve at influencing both the circumstances and the people involved.

Finally, sticky leaders know that since none of us have reached this vision for a new reality, everyone will need to learn together what it takes to lean into the new future. This is where Learning to Love Uphill gets critically important.

---

7   If you would like to learn more about the Vision to Action (V2A) leadership model visit www.V2A.com/LeadershipModel

LEAD OTHERS by CREATING ATTRACTIVE CHANGE

What frustrates you the most about leading others? When I ask my clients this question, I often get answers like these:

"When they disappoint me."

"When people let me down."

"When they just don't get it."

"When someone doesn't follow through."

"When I can't seem to get my people to do what I want them to."

"When they say one thing and do another."

"When people seem to give up."

"The amount of time it takes. People, for me, are a lot of work."

Sticky leadership works from the inside out, which means it begins with us, then moves to leading in the situation, and finally to leading others. When we approach our leadership in this way, something significant changes . . . as do our frustrations with leading others.

A Natural Attraction

How do sticky leaders approach leading others? For one thing, they lead differently than many old-style guides would suggest.

Non-sticky leadership often involves using a strategy of effective team building techniques, or developing a system that benevolently manipulates followers into doing something the leader wants done. But in truth, this old way of thinking about leadership is not very sticky.

The beauty of sticky leadership is that it acts like a magnet, attracting the right people to join the leadership team to bring some compelling vision into reality. The right people are literally drawn into roles that allow them to both follow and lead. It is a natural thing, rather than some sort of a strategy or kindly manipulation. In fact, the authenticity of sticky leadership is the very thing that makes it work.

Remember the axiom that *an inspiring vision, powerfully spoken, that becomes shared, will pull for its own fulfillment?* This includes attracting those who will want to help in the work of Loving Uphill. In this chapter, I want to discuss how to use the pull of vision and the sharing of commitment as the attractant and glue to build a leadership team that functions well together.

I've observed that people feel highly attracted to sticky leaders and naturally want to learn from them. The men and women so drawn also want to know how the leader has such influence over circumstances. "How is it you can behave in a way that appears so effortless?" they ask. "Why don't you get frustrated and angry like others? And how did you get so good at converting obstacles into breakthroughs?"

When people feel drawn to you in this way, you are ready to lead others. Until then, keep practicing self-leadership and leading the circumstances. Trust me, at some point, people will begin to show up, wanting to learn from you or receive your help in becoming more like you, so that they can lead their own circumstances.

A Sticky Leader Par Excellence

As I've mentioned, the first sticky leader I ever met was the president and founder of Timberline Software, John Gorman. When those of us who worked under John's leadership in the late '70s and '80s talk about the old days, the conversation inevitably moves to our love and respect for him. We all sensed something incredible about John and about the way he touched so many lives. Each of us had similar experiences of him, even though we all played very different roles in the company.

Timberline was an innovator in the packaged software industry, known especially for its accounting products. We all believed we were building something important (the circumstances), which bonded us together, and we universally admired John as our leader. The way he operated seemed so natural and effortless.

What is it about John that made him stand out? When you talk to individuals who had the pleasure of experiencing his leadership, you continually hear things like these:

- He trusted me to a fault.

- He really knew us, remembered our names and our family members.

- I couldn't really tell you what he did as president, other than spend time with his people.

- He knew the product, the business, and our customers in a way you couldn't BS him.

- He was an amazingly good judge of people.

- He was sensitive to others. I can't remember him saying an unkind word about anyone, although he always was candid about performance and failures.

- He had a self-deprecating sense of humor.

- He was wise. You could ask him about anything and you could expect to get some valuable insight or a question asked back at you that you could chew on for days.

- He was painfully honest about everything.

- He had high standards.

- He didn't expect perfection, only your very best.

- You would leave a meeting with him with the uncanny sense that he knew you better than you knew yourself.

- He was optimistic and at the same time pragmatic.

- He would make big requests of you that felt enormously challenging, but you had a sense that he believed you could accomplish them (even when you had some doubts about yourself).

- He loved his family and was a man of faith.

As the oldest of nine children, I felt a special connection with John, since he had nine kids himself. At times, he seemed more like a father figure to me than my boss. I learned more about sticky leadership from John than I probably learned from anyone else. He became my model for sticky leadership, and his example still informs my perspective today.

Most importantly, perhaps, John's sticky leadership rubbed off on a large number of the leaders he influenced. His influence lives on today in leaders across the country who took up the banner of sticky leadership, a vision that he first planted in our souls.

What's in the Secret Sauce?

So what's the secret to how sticky leaders transfer these leadership qualities and abilities to others? What magical ingredients do they put in their secret sauce? I've noticed at least seven consistent patterns in their behavior.

1. **Sticky leaders practice self-leadership.**

    These leaders model behaviors consistent with what they say. They exude integrity and have a humble quality about them that makes them both safe and interesting to learn from.

2. **Sticky leaders influence their circumstances, both in their personal life and on the grander stage.**

    Sticky leaders have big visions and aren't shy about sharing them. Because of this, they attract like-minded people. In fact, people tend to flock around them.

3. **Sticky leaders are genuinely likable and consistently show that they like and value others.**

    Hanging around sticky leaders brings its own rewards. There is something attractive about them that draws others like moths to a light bulb, even if these leaders aren't highly relational. People see value in hanging around them because they see something about them that makes a difference in life.

4. **Sticky leaders take the time to learn about others.**

    They're always asking questions that demonstrate a genuine interest in their people: "How are you?" "How is your son?" "How did the camping trip go last weekend?" They much prefer asking about the welfare of others than they care to talk about themselves.

5. **Sticky leaders naturally transfer to others the essence of who they are and what they know.**

    They don't have some handbook that they follow or some system that they use; they simply make the transfer in a natural, organic way. It's just part of who they are.

6. **Sticky leaders know how to invite others to participate in the vision.**

   This invitation may come in subtle or very direct ways, but sticky leaders continually add members to the team and have a way of keeping them once they come on board, even when things get difficult.

7. **Sticky leaders model and practice what they preach.**

   Sticky leaders act consistently in ways that keep them sharp, engaged, and actively doing whatever it takes to shift the circumstances in favor of the vision.

Really, there's no "secret sauce" that explains the almost magical power that sticky leaders wield. They succeed because they want everyone on their team to succeed together in an adventure worth pursuing. Their passion, humility, enthusiasm and genuine concern rub off on everyone in their orbit. And success just has a way of following them around.

It's Just That Simple

In essence, inside out leadership means that sticky leaders constantly attract people who want to know what the leader knows and how to do what the leader does. People find great value by getting close to them and by engaging with them to bring some potent vision into reality.

Sticky leaders don't seem to have a particular formula for how they lead. Very simply, they just have a consistent, positive influence over those they attract, especially those who join their team.

The sticky leadership model of leading others is just that simple.

Part Three

A GAME WORTH PLAYING

For leadership to become sticky, it has to be replicated in and through others; otherwise, it's just exceptional personal performance masquerading as leadership. Leaders without followers are just kidding themselves. Their impact will be limited in scope by what they can accomplish on their own.

In my years of working intimately with leaders, I've found the most difficult part of developing sticky leadership always involves the process: How do I get my influence to stick? How can I replicate what I am? Any number of books written by leadership experts will give you tips and techniques about developing followers. But here's a crucial difference between the sticky leadership approach and others: I call it, "Creating a Game worth Playing."

Sticky leaders have a knack for inviting others to play a game worth playing. They know how to call out the best in their followers. When I use the game analogy, I'm not trivializing the leadership process; just the opposite, in fact. I use the metaphor to picture a highly effective way of thinking about how great leadership calls people to get involved. A Game worth Playing offers helpful insight about honoring the intensity and attention to rules and details that are always required to win games. Games can be both serious and playful at the same time. All good games are engaging and require a measure of skill to win. It takes time to become a master at any game, so persistence is important.

Business is a lot like that. And so the familiar experience of playing games provides leaders with several key insights into achieving sustainability as they apply Uphill energy to move current reality toward their vision.

FIND A GAME WORTH PLAYING

My dad, an accountant, used to look at work as a game. Along with a few other partners, his name appeared on the door of a successful CPA firm. But his name came last on the door, which is where I think he landed in the pecking order.

His partners had their offices on the top floor of the two-story building they built and rented out to other professionals, while Dad's office sat on the bottom floor. I never asked him about the apparent disparity of his being a partner in the firm and yet not having a top floor office, and he never gave me any indication that it bothered him.

Dad may have worked on the bottom floor, but his clients highly respected him. I believe he got a great deal more personal satisfaction from their respect than he would have from hanging out on the top floor. The seated governor was one of his clients, for example, and each year my dad prepared the governor's tax return. The opening day of fishing season often fell on the day after tax season ended, a very busy time for my dad. I barely saw him then, but I did see the governor and his son, fishing off our dock on Wards Lake in Olympia, Washington. The sight gave a very clear message to all of us kids: We had a very important dad.

Dad often described accounting and preparing tax returns in a way that surprised me. He would call it "fun," like solving a puzzle for his clients. He clearly enjoyed his work and I believe he was really good at what he did.

Even back at home, when he and I would work in our large vegetable garden, he would arrange my chores—which I really didn't look forward to—as games to play, after which I would receive some sort of a reward (even if it amounted to just the satisfaction of a job well done).

Those early experiences set my mind down a lifelong track of thinking about work and business as a Game worth Playing. I've found this perspective adds a powerful and invaluable dimension to equipping yourself for success, especially at those times when you feel like giving up or when you need something extra to achieve sustainability. I have used this frame of thinking for more than twenty-five years of coaching executives, and I know it works.

The Power of Games

People like to play games and they always have. Some experts think the game of Mancala has won devoted players for about 7,000 years. Ancient Egyptians drew pictures of their board games on limestone walls. Today, games are big business. In 2010, people spent more than $25 billion dollars on video games alone. Yes, people like to play games.

You can find almost an infinite number of games out there—individual games, group games, games of chance, games of endurance, games of skill, computer games, board games, and games of pure fun. We enjoy watching people playing games, and we like teaching others how to play the games we know and love.

COACHING CORNER

Wht games do you most like to play?

What makes those games fun for you?

So what makes games so attractive? Why do we like them so much? Or more to the point: What do you like about games? On the following list, how many of the items are true for you about the games you enjoy?

- Games have a specific beginning, middle and end
- Playing games is a matter of choice
- We play games for fun and our own purposes
- Games have a way of keeping score so we know how we're doing against the competition
- Games have seasons or rounds of play. If we finish poorly in one, we get to start over with a clean scorecard and try again
- Some games are social and some are solitary. We get to pick the kind we like
- Games can help us better understand ourselves and others
- Games involve learning by doing, which fits our human nature
- If we choose, we can get good at games we like
- Games are viewed as play, as opposed to work; we play for fun
- Games challenge us, sometimes in surprising ways
- Games provide their own rewards, like winning and the thrill of competing

As you think of games you like to play, what other features of game play do you enjoy? Why do you keep playing certain games? If you ever recruit others to play your favorite games, how do you try to get them interested enough to try those games?

The Four Key Elements

In business, four key elements go into identifying and creating a Game worth Playing. Those four elements are as follows:

1. Create an elevating purpose, directly connected to the vision, that everyone can easily embrace.

2. Identify a clear goal or outcome (everyone wants to know how we win!).

3. Develop rules of play that, when followed, give us the opportunity to win.

4. Define a season of play with a clear beginning, middle, and end.

Let's see how one company applied these four steps to help them turn around a difficult situation.

Step One: Create an Elevating Purpose

One client who specializes in construction services had two challenges going on at once. First, it lacked any real profitability, despite growing top-line revenues driven by a healthy investment in sales and marketing. Its people worked harder and harder for little to no reward. Second, its employees did not appear to trust each other, and as a result, they failed to make necessary corporate changes. And that left them stuck.

The business already had a vision: "A company consistently profitable at every level, with employees who are honest, transparent, and fully engaged in making the business enduringly successful." What elevating purpose could connect with this vision? Key leadership in the company agreed, "Our purpose is to make the work we do for our customers a satisfying and rewarding experience for all." Of course, this included the employees, while "satisfying" included quality, profitability, and return customers.

The important process of developing this vision and purpose (or vision and mission) got people talking about the experience of working for the company, which provided both fuel (think energy) and validation for the Game worth Playing.

Step Two: Identify a Clear Goal

The company needed a goal that would focus everyone on winning and provide everyone with great clarity about the desired outcome of the game. They made it their goal to achieve 5 percent profitability by the end of the next quarter. They also identified a secondary goal: At each weekly leadership meeting, they would check in on their corporate values of honesty and transparency, both with themselves and the customer. They promised to share customer stories and feedback with one another at each meeting.

As they tested their ideas week by week, they refined their measurements and improved their processes. The "win" they sought was happy customers, a profitable business, and increasing employee engagement, as measured by honest and transparent conversations.

Step Three: Develop Rules of Play

Developing the rules of play took a bit more thinking. They had to look at how the business operated and then target whatever got in the way of profitability. They soon discovered that often they didn't follow their own price book, usually out of fear that they wouldn't make their sales goals without offering competitive discounts. But once they realized they were working harder for no real benefit or profitability, they decided that sticking to their own values and pricing would be a smarter way to play the game.

They also put another rule in place, supported by something they called a "Social Covenant" that directed everyone in the company to treat each other with truth, honesty, and respect. This covenant took a few all-hands meetings to hammer out and became the foundation of a playbook that could grow and evolve over time. Everyone who had a hand in assembling the social covenant also signed it, thus promising to abide by it. The covenant included a process to follow if someone forgot their commitment, designed to help get them back on track.

Step Four: Determine the Season of Play
The company originally targeted three months as a realistic period of play, but eventually decided to create a first half and second half period of play, each lasting three months. As a group, they planned a big kick-off event and began to think about how they would celebrate the end of the season in six months. This was enough to get them started.

As they played the game, they learned a great deal about old habits and weaknesses that they had to refine to better play the game. As they challenged each other to remain honest and transparent, the culture of the business began to change and everyone started to feel more ownership in the results the company achieved. Over time, their situation improved—and in the process, they found themselves having a lot more fun.

Once an organization completes a season of play, it makes a great deal of sense to plan a celebration. Have fun, but also harvest the meaning of what happened and identify what you learned from the season so that you can do it all over again.

Your Personal Game worth Playing

The process of creating a Game worth Playing follows the pattern of leading from the inside out. Self-leadership, therefore, means that we do this for ourselves first. So then—what is your personal Game worth Playing? What makes Learning to Love Uphill a worthy focus of your energy?

I can tell you personally that when the obvious rewards of bringing my vision into reality don't materialize as quickly as I intend them to, I have to look for deeper reasons to stay engaged in the Uphill journey. To find these deeper reasons, it helps me to ask searching questions that uncover the deepest desires of my heart and identify the lasting difference I want to make in the world.

To clarify your own Game worth Playing, ask yourself a few questions. Recognize that these questions go to the heart of who you are as a person:

- What makes life worth living for you?
- When you feel most joyful, what are you doing? What have you accomplished?
- What do you feel most proud of, even when no one is looking?
- What do you most want to accomplish in this life? Why?
- What would you like to give back to others that you yourself have received?
- If you died today, what would you want written on your tombstone?
- What do you want to be remembered for, long after you're gone?

If you take these questions seriously and put your answers at the heart of your own Game worth Playing, you will bring a huge measure of significance to your Uphill journey. So spend some real effort identifying your personal Game worth Playing, one that captures the meaning and significance of what you just identified. Target the joy and fun of the journey!

Years ago I found a quote by Robert S. de Ropp that captures the spirit of what I've tried to describe. Linger over these words as you ponder a suitable Game worth Playing for yourself:

> *Seek, above all, for a game worth playing. Such is the advice of the oracle to modern man. Having found the game, play*

it with intensity—play as if your life and sanity depended on it. (They do depend on it.) Follow the example of the French existentialists and flourish a banner bearing the word "engagement." Though nothing means anything and all roads are marked "NO EXIT," yet move as if your movements had some purpose. If life does not seem to offer a game worth playing, then invent one. For it must be clear, even to the most clouded intelligence, that any game is better than no game.

It truly is better to have some game rather than no game. And when things get most difficult, it helps to know that even if this particular effort fails, you can always begin again with a new game, a new season, and even with a new team. This will help you to keep things from getting too heavy and serious, even though you remain committed to winning to the very end. Once you do this for yourself, you can begin to help others recognize their own personal Game worth Playing.

Gaining the Right Mindset

To obtain the Game worth Playing mindset for your business or career, first consider the games you like to play. Why and how do you play them? Notice how you make time for enjoying these games, even early on when you have to do the laborious work of learning their rules and practicing to become a good player.

After that comes the challenge of competition, either with yourself or with others. You don't win every time you play; and yet, once you finish a game, you're often ready to play again. How many times have you sat with friends, playing some fun game, when the hour grew late and someone said, "Let's play just one more?" Invariably another person said, "Why not?" and you continued despite the late hour.

This kind of thinking begins to capture the sense of creating a Game worth Playing in your leadership efforts, and then helping others to learn to do the same. We see so many parallels and powerful analogies between playing games and skilled leadership that it is worth studying in depth. Without question, this perspective has sustained me in difficult seasons more times than I can count.

When you add to this mindset the idea of seasons of play and the ability to begin a fresh season with a clean record after failing miserably, you can begin to grasp the enormous value of consciously crafting and perfecting a personal Game worth Playing in regard to your career or business. This mindset helps to shift the concept of risk and the "matter of life and death" thinking that can accompany the tough challenges you face in creating the breakthroughs you need.

If you examine the attractive and powerful concept of games and pay attention to the games you like playing, you can gain powerful insights that will help you to sustain your energy in the face of Uphill challenges.

So how can you create your own Game worth Playing? Imagine this as a process of finding two key elements. These two companion elements are:

- Meaning
- Fun

Let's begin with the first element, meaning. How do you find the meaning in your Game worth Playing as you take an Uphill journey to your breakthrough?

Find the Meaning

Just as world-class athletes striving for excellence look to the bigger personal meaning behind their sports as the force that drives them, so you need to search for the meaning behind your breakthrough. Once you find it, embrace that meaning for yourself and then find ways to help others do the same. Purpose has power. When individuals know why they are doing something and they identify with that purpose, they can tap the necessary effort to make it happen. Let me give you an example from the business world.

A natural fiber window coverings company had been struggling for years to get past a sales volume and profitability plateau. Leadership soon identified the breakthrough they needed: The company had to become more skillful in recognizing market trends and desires, while simultaneously becoming more skillful in the ways they used creative talent to design more profitable products.

In the process of crafting its Game worth Playing, the company recognized that its business provided a livelihood for people in Asia who harvested, prepared, and pre-manufactured the resources the company then used to craft into beautiful products sold through designers to upscale buyers in America. This realization led the company to uncover more of the stories of its employees and associates, making those stories a key part of its corporate brand identity.

Suddenly, the meaning of this company's Game worth Playing connected very personally to everyone in its business ecosphere, not only to those who helped the firm acquire the necessary resources, but also to the designers who took those beautiful raw materials and used their skills to create living environments that felt restful, comfortable, and even healing to eager consumers. This discovery fueled the efforts of everyone in the company, energizing them to reach out to individuals on both ends of the supply and business chain. They purposefully worked to connect their designs to their profitability.

As you look at your own business, what meaning do you find there? What element can you identify that has the power to fuel the efforts of everyone in your company, energizing them to reach out to people both within and outside of your company?

Find the Fun

With the meaning of your Game identified, next you need to find the fun and rewarding part. What joyful attraction can help you to achieve the purpose behind your vision?

Let's be honest; not everything in the Uphill journey is fun, meaningful, or even seemingly worthwhile. That's why at the heart of sustainability lies the idea of locating these experiences in the bigger context of a Game worth Playing. The primary object here is to identify and get in touch with the strongest source of motivation behind the leadership commitment areas that define your vision. Finding the fun in what you do can take some work, and in part it has to do with the way you think.

In twenty-five years of working with entrepreneurs and their teams, I've found that the fun usually comes from doing what you're good at. You have the most fun when you use your gifts and talents to make a positive difference. Your breakthrough, in fact, will most likely come as a result of doing what you are good at and helping others to do the same. What parts of the Game bring you the most enjoyment and rewards? As the leader, think of yourself as the Game Master; it's your job to help your people see the fun aspects of the Game and enjoy them. They might not find those areas of enjoyment without your help and leadership!

Throughout history, great leaders have modeled this strategy of creating a Game worth Playing. Each of the following well known historical events were led by men and women who created a Game worth Playing that sharpened their focus and attracted followers. I count this list of leaders and their "games" as among my favorites:

- Dr. Martin Luther King and equality (the civil rights game worth playing)
- Abraham Lincoln and unity (the civil war resolution game worth playing)

- George Washington and freedom (the battle of independence game worth playing)
- John F. Kennedy and the space race (the first man to the moon game worth playing)
- Florence Nightingale and the professionalization of nursing (the nursing-as-an-honorable-profession game worth playing)
- Marie Curie and the discovery of radiation as a therapeutic tool (the radioactivity game worth playing)
- Steve Jobs and the Apple Computer (the insanely great products game worth playing)

For a sticky leader, it's fun to overcome a challenge that seemed nearly impossible. It's fun to do something that causes people to smile. It's fun to enable teams to succeed, to create beautiful or useful products that consumers love, to improve the life of a forgotten worker in faraway Asia.

Just recently, Howard Schultz of Starbucks announced a plan that would enable every Starbucks employee (he calls them "partners") to get a college education, tuition free. The official Starbucks website declares,

> Starbucks believes in the promise and pursuit of the American Dream. In a first of its kind collaboration with Arizona State University, we're offering all part- and full-time benefits eligible U.S. partners the opportunity to receive 100 percent tuition coverage–for all four years–to earn a bachelor's degree. Partners may choose from nearly 50 undergraduate degree programs through ASU's research driven and top-ranked program, delivered online.

That's an ambitious program, and no doubt it will cost Starbucks a mountain of cash. Critics already have carped about this or that feature of the plan, and almost certainly the company will have to make some changes to the program along the way. But here's the thing: Do you think Howard Schultz had fun putting it together? Do you think he had fun announcing it to the world? Do you think he enjoyed the idea of doing something special for the people who make Starbucks such a global force?

Find a Game worth Playing and then have some fun with it.

Attract and Retain Players

Leadership is not a solo game. By definition, leaders have followers and part of your Game worth Playing has to focus on attracting and retaining players. Easier said than done!

In my years of coaching executives, attracting and retaining the right players is probably among the top three frustrations I commonly hear. That frustration gets expressed in different ways:

- Why won't these people just do what I say?
- If only they were as passionate about this vision as I am!
- The turnover here is killing us.
- It's hard to find people who think the way I do.
- If only they were better leaders! But they are control freaks who do everything themselves.
- Why don't they get it? It seems so obvious to me.
- I wish they would show some ownership.

Attracting and retaining followers has to be part of the game plan for a sticky leader. Then there must be some sort of a connection between you and those playing the game in order to facilitate a transfer of thinking, a sharing of values, and the cultivation of mutual interest in learning how to play the game together. The glue that connects this is best defined as love. It seems odd to talk about love and leadership in the same breath, but I have no better way of describing it.

The sticky leader has to love the game and love the players who join him or her. And that love must be felt by all those engaged in the Uphill journey.

Leaders often fail right here. When I hear complaints like those listed above, I begin some detective work. I talk with "the players" and check to see if they feel a connection with their leader. If I see no emotional connection, I know that all the things most important to the leader will not get transferred to the organization. The required "stickiness" just isn't there.

So how do you attract the right players to your game and then retain them? How do you create enough stickiness to transfer the crucial things to both the heads and hearts of your followers? You have to commit yourself to the following:

- Make up your mind to love your people unconditionally.
- Let your people know you appreciate them.
- Ask for the opinions and ideas of others before you give your own.
- Learn and use your people's names.
- Take time to learn the personal visions of others.
- Access your heart as much as your head.
- Be kind, never mean.
- Keep an open mind and practice persuasion (not coercion).
- Honor the values of others without compromising your own.
- Ask for and offer help.
- Apologize when appropriate.
- Practice your faith.

Players know when they are loved and appreciated. The tough thing is that this can't be faked. It takes a serious commitment to develop a heart for those who choose to join you in the Game worth Playing.

My Own Game worth Playing

My first business turnaround experience in Guam gave me my own story about creating a Game worth Playing. In my mid-twenties, I moved to Guam to manage a computer service bureau after I completed active duty with the U.S. Navy. I had worked part time for this company during my Navy stint in Guam, and I knew it had some business problems that I thought I might be able to resolve. When the company offered me partial ownership in the business, my wife and I landed in Guam with one-way tickets to launch this great new adventure.

One week later, I discovered to my dismay that things in the company were far worse than I had imagined. The company was literally bankrupt and didn't even know it. The owners had worked themselves into a financial hole that looked almost impossible to dig out of.

Much to our advantage at the time, no one else on the island provided our type of business accounting services. That gave us time to see if we could work our way back to profitability. Part of the challenge of making the necessary business improvements was to attract the talent we needed to grow and improve the company. Unfortunately, because computers were still relatively new in Guam and the island had a relatively small pool of available workers, we did not have many talented recruits from which to choose. I found myself training individuals with the needed aptitude, but since I couldn't pay them a competitive wage, once they got trained and confident, they moved down the street to work for a competitor. This frustrated me to no end, as I always seemed to be in training mode and could never retain good talent. I couldn't blame them, though; we simply did not have the funds to pay them what they were worth.

Eventually I started telling candidates, up front, that while they would be underpaid as our employees, they would learn valuable skills that they could use later to get better paying jobs. I had little choice but to embrace our current reality. It seemed like the only way I could keep our struggling business going.

Then something unusual happened. I had a shift of perspective that relates to creating a Game worth Playing. I finally decided that my Game was to become the best computer talent training company on the island. Once I did that, my irritation with people leaving subsided. We got pretty good at training people and getting them up to speed before they left to go down the street. It helped that when people left, they thanked me for what they had accomplished and for all they had learned. That made me feel good and helped me to see the larger picture of what we were doing—upgrading computer skills all across the island. In the meantime, our business continued to make headway on becoming more healthy and profitable.

Another turning point occurred when I hired a new computer operator named Tom, who told me all about his personal aspirations. He wanted to become a gemologist, a career track that eventually would require a move to Hawaii, where he could get appropriate schooling. I let him know that I was on his team and that when he had earned enough money to leave Guam, I would gladly send him off, knowing I had supported his personal career vision.

Tom stayed with me for three years, even though he could have gone down the street and made more money elsewhere. Making more money would have hastened his departure to gemology school. So why did Tom stay?

I think he remained because Tom and I shared a common vision. We both wanted him to succeed down the road as a gemologist in Hawaii, and we both wanted my company to succeed as a profitable business that could pay competitive wages and retain good employees. This shared vision led directly to a Game worth Playing. Tom eventually did leave after he had saved up enough money. We had a great celebration on his departure, because after all, we had won!

A few years later, when I departed Guam after successfully turning around the company—by then, I could finally pay my people a competitive wage and they had begun to stick around—I stopped in Hawaii to visit Tom. He was working as a gemologist in an upscale jewelry store where he designed his own products. Not only did I have fun seeing Tom living out his vision, but the fulfillment of the Game worth Playing for each of us amounted to a great reward, in and of itself.

The process of creating a Game worth Playing leads to intimacy. I learned about Tom's dreams for his future and I found a sympathetic ear to listen to my frustrations and hear about my vision for creating a healthy and profitable company with a stable workforce. When leaders get to know their people in this way, they create a sort of leadership stickiness that provides both the glue and the motivation to achieve whatever is required to create breakthroughs.

The Growth Game

Entrepreneurs often ask me about growing their businesses. They want to know, "Should I grow this just to make it bigger, or should I have some other reason?" I usually respond, "It depends," and then I begin to ask questions probing for the person's personal Game worth Playing. I know we've hit on something when the individual lights up and gets excited.

Growth for growth's sake doesn't typically provide sufficient material for a Game worth Playing. Therefore it pays to continue to reflect on what you consider most important. What gets you up in the morning? What do you want to be remembered for after you leave this planet? What makes it all fun and rewarding for you to find and play a Game worth Playing?

Once you've identified your own Game worth Playing, you can use it to make each day memorable, whether you win, lose or draw. It helps you to remember what's at stake, to know that you can't recover the day you just spent, and to choose to make the most of every day by growing something important for both yourself and for others.

You can think of the growth game like this: "What do I lack in my life? What do my loved ones need more of right now and in the future?" Some of my entrepreneurial clients tell me they need more time—time with their family, more time doing the things they enjoy. Then their growth game is creating a Game worth Playing that gives them more time, not only for themselves, but also for others, including employees and customers. Such a choice tends to aim the growth game at greater streamlining and efficiency.

So what's your own Game worth Playing? What do you lack that you need? What do you or your loved ones need more of, right now and in the future? You'll know it when you identify it, because your eyes will light up, you'll speak in a more animated way, and the very idea of playing that game—whatever it is—will excite you down to your toes.

And that's why it's worth playing.

COACH in a GAME WORTH PLAYING

Great game players seldom achieve their amazing success without great coaching. "A coach is someone who can give correction without causing resentment," said the late John Wooden, the legendary UCLA men's basketball coach. His record of NCAA championships will likely never get broken. And Vince Lombardi, the equally legendary NFL coach, once declared, "Coaches who can outline plays on a black board are a dime a dozen. The ones who win get inside their players and motivate." Lombardi did that. That's why he won. And that's why he's legendary.

Sticky leaders view themselves as leadership coaches. Once they've identified the right Game worth Playing, coaching becomes a natural practice for them.

Understand People so You Can Coach Them

By definition, creating breakthroughs requires that everyone involved learns to face the unknown and play the game with abandon, doing the best they know how. Coaching is a way of bringing out the best in each of us. Getting good results requires practice and a genuine interest in people, understanding what makes them tick.

All of us are uniquely and wonderfully made. No two humans are genetically identical. Even monozygotic twins, who develop from a single zygote, have slight genetic differences, due primarily to mutations occurring during development.

Our differences, of course, extend beyond just our genetic makeup. No two people have the same fingerprints. In fact, no two fingers, not even on the same person, are alike. Although we are all made up of the same chemical and biophysical ingredients, each of us is unique. Only one blueprint led to you.

Add to those physical differences our natural gifts and personality differences, our own set of personal life experiences, and our cultural differences, and it seems extremely odd to me that we would treat any two people the same. But I see leaders do this all the time.

A prerequisite to effective coaching is to recognize the uniqueness of the individual we are coaching. Sticky leadership requires that we match our approach to the individual. Certainly, we share common patterns and we tend to react similarly in many situations; but sticky leaders never lose sight of the uniqueness of each person they coach.

Our Assumptions Can Get Us in Trouble

As an executive coach, I have seen a leader's unexamined assumptions lead to many serious mistakes. We've already looked at one common faulty assumption, namely, that people are eerily similar and can be treated in essentially the same way. Making such broad generalizations misses the heart of effective coaching, which requires the coach to connect with the uniqueness of each individual.

We sometimes make another mistake by assuming that we know what is going on inside of people, without taking the time to actually inquire and hear about their true thoughts and feelings. Assumptions kill us when we're trying to uncover someone's true motivations.

I remember a story about a business owner who had hired a woman to work in the customer service department.

Right from the beginning, she seemed to grasp the work and customers really liked her. Over the course of a few weeks, however, she consistently arrived late to work and seemed distracted on the job. Another employee complained about having to cover for her in her absence. In a short time, morale started to decline in the department. The manager had one brief conversation with her, warning her to get to work on time. When she continued to arrive late, the manager concluded she had lost her commitment to the job and just didn't care enough to get to work on time. He knew she was a single mom and needed the money, but her poor performance had begun hurting the business.

When he summoned her into his office to give his final warning, she broke down in tears. She finally admitted that she had lost her babysitter for her young son and couldn't find a replacement. In the meantime, her mother was helping out, but she had to drive some distance to leave the child in her care. She felt deeply embarrassed by the situation and didn't know what else to do. She had begun to lose hope that she could find a replacement at all and the long drive to her mother's home added to the difficulty and to her frustration.

"Would you be willing to share your situation with your co-workers?" her manager asked. He wanted to see if they could help her find a solution and work as a team to cover the department's customer service needs until she could come up with a better solution. She did so, and the eventual solution came from one of her co-workers who knew someone looking for work. That person became a perfect fit.

In this scenario, all kinds of erroneous interpretations were taking place simultaneously. The embarrassed young woman had avoided talking about her circumstances for fear of losing her job. Her boss had labeled her a slacker, despite her early job success. Her co-workers had made their own interpretations about her commitment to the job, based on their frustrations over having to cover for her. Only the manager's last ditch meeting brought out the truth, when the woman finally broke down in tears. Only then did everyone start working on the real situation, rather than on what they had imagined.

The lesson? Our assumptions will get us into trouble almost every time. Don't trust them! Do what you can to find out. Ask rather than assume, which may require you to become vulnerable and honest. As leaders, we must lead with compassion, even in situations where emotions run high and when we think we know what's happening. We often discover surprises that can lead to breakthroughs, or at least the removal of a few kinks in the hose.

The Fundamental Design Construct for Coaching

It would take a lifetime of scientific research to truly understand the unique differences between individuals, but for the purposes of leadership and coaching, we can use a select set of distinctions to try to understand a framework for those differences, relative to effective coaching. At least four distinctions can provide sticky leaders with a great deal of help when shifting into the coaching mode.

1. **The source of motivation**

    Why do people do what they do? Any discussion about human motivation must take into account the study of Abraham Maslow and his "hierarchy of needs." In 1943, Maslow wrote a paper titled Theory of Human Motivation in which he examined the concept that a hierarchical ladder of human needs can help us to understand what motivates people. At the lowest level, humans are motivated by mere survival. As each need is met while moving up the ladder, a higher level need serves as the activating motivational force.

For decades, Maslow's theory has been regarded as useful in both the field of psychology and in business, and certainly in America, where our most fundamental needs can be met with relative ease (compared to those in developing world countries where survival is a daily concern). Often we find ourselves in the highest category defined by Maslow, which is "self-actualization." In this arena, we access our personal and spiritual purpose and try to live it out.

Two key concepts help us to define both our source of motivation and the fundamental capacity to fulfill our purpose in life. Our vision of an ideal future and our true design, based on our core values, lie at the root of our intrinsic motivation. These two concepts represent two sides of the same coin, the coin of accomplishment. This "coin of the realm" literally represents the currency of our capacity to live out our life purpose. Both of these concepts represent the fuel and the ability to do what is required and to become who we were made to be.

2. Inspiring Personal Vision

For over a quarter of a century, I have researched the role that vision plays in enabling individuals and organizations to fulfill their purpose and destiny. I have concluded that an inspiring personal vision is critical to pursuing a self-actualized life.

Every vision is rooted in a set of key commitment areas. A true commitment area is a subject of supreme importance, such that a person will invest both their time and resources to pursue it. Common key commitment areas include health, wealth, family, friends, faith, career, community, learning, and so on. Key commitment areas become the main sources of reserve energy that you can tap to pursue an ideal outcome.

As an executive coach, I have found that surfacing and honoring the top level key commitment areas (generally four of them), and helping my clients to clearly articulate a vision of the future for each of them, becomes a clear and powerful form of motivation.

3. Shared Vision

When vision develops collectively and in a way that encourages a large natural overlap between personal visions and a shared vision, group motivation skyrockets. In fact, a shared vision, powerfully spoken, will pull for its own fulfillment. Two of my favorite shared visions from history are the vision for racial equality spoken by Dr. Martin Luther King, which became shared by the racial equality movement he successfully led, and the vision to put a man on the moon before the end of the 1960s, spoken by President John F. Kennedy in 1961. Great visions often become more powerful than the person speaking them (Kennedy died in 1963, while Neil Armstrong stepped on the surface of the moon in 1969) and galvanize large numbers of people to take the actions necessary to make the vision happen.

4. Core Values

Each of us has a unique set of core values that guides our behaviors. We cannot authentically act differently than our core values; that's simply how we are made. Sustained, ongoing success comes in large part by how well we live out our core values. Any of us can fake it for a period of time, but our natural tendencies eventually will make themselves known.

Our vision and values are perfectly coordinated to work in harmony, reflecting the beauty of our design. In years of coaching, I have found a profound symmetry between the vision of a person's soul (what he feels most called to invest his life in) and the values underlying how the individual is fundamentally wired. As a coach, I help people recognize this symmetry and then give themselves permission to live out the life they believe they were made to live. One of the reasons sticky leadership works is that it takes into consideration the true nature of the person. It accurately connects what is true for each person to the Game worth Playing.

A big vision provides a multitude of roles to fill, and the sticky leader understands how to connect people with the unique contribution they can make. This is more of a matching process than a grooming process. In professional sports, when a team needs to fill a particular position, it begins searching for a player with the specific attributes it needs. It looks for a match. The same concept holds in sticky leadership, which makes it different from some traditional leadership practices that rely on manipulation to get people to do what the Game requires.

Value: Type of Energy

We looked earlier at the different types of energy each person brings to the process of Loving Uphill. In reality, the preferred types of energy a person brings to the Game typically align with the values of that person.

The four fundamental categories of value are Power, Love, Wisdom and Knowledge. Lynn Taylor connected these four core values to each main type of energy. His Core Values Index (CVI) assessment tool can be used to effectively measure an individual's relative distribution between these four values. This unique mix of values is what defines us and catalyzes the vision each of us has for the future. It helps us to define the best way to strategically use our energy to bring a vision into reality. Leadership energy connects to each of these four core values in the following way:

- Power: Action and Results Building
- Love: Relationship Building and Maintenance
- Wisdom: Problem Solving and Innovation
- Knowledge: Information Collection and Stewardship

The values of a leader connect with the most natural actions of that leader. This values/energy matrix suggests the role that an individual can most effectively play on a team.

Power = Results
A person with the value of power likes feeling personally powerful. These individuals get things done to bring about the breakthrough; they know how to put people into action. In the Game worth Playing, leaders always need this kind of person. You can envision him as a quarterback, calling the plays and getting the agreements required to move the action down the field of play.

Love = Human Sensitivity
Someone with the value of love has a natural interest in people and has a keen awareness of the human dynamic. This value perfectly positions this individual in roles where understanding people, connecting with them, and serving them comes naturally. This value automatically brings a "future possibility" consciousness, particularly when it comes to relationships and what can be accomplished in and through people. You want to put individuals with this value on the front lines of dealing with others to get things done, particularly when it involves persuasion or problem solving with those both inside and outside of the company.

Wisdom = Problem Solving

Any breakthrough always has a multitude of problems to solve, and since the situation keeps changing every day, new problems come to light every day. Those who value wisdom take delight in the opportunity to solve these problems, and they're naturally good at it. Imagine how effective one can be in the Game worth Playing if problems actually energize him or her! Again, good coaching uncovers personal values and can be used to skillfully engage the people who value wisdom, putting them in roles where they can thrive by solving problems. In that way, they gladly contribute to winning the Game.

Knowledge = Honoring and Using Information

Although we live in the information age, not all of us have a natural affinity for collecting, referencing and honoring the information that controls and influences the Game. Those with the value of knowledge are natural stewards of information and enjoy collecting and sharing it with others for the common good. They tend to have a conservative cautiousness aimed at protecting everyone involved in the Game. They also love to honor the rules of engagement (which we'll discuss in the final chapter).

A Natural Way to Win

Sticky leaders recognize and honor values because they know that understanding the values of their teammates in the Game allows them to tap into their teammates' natural motivation. And they know that everyone wins when everybody feels motivated to succeed.

By living our values, we add value to any game we play. Coaching brings value by recognizing and honoring the values of others, which (as a side benefit) builds trust among team members.

As I write, Mike Krzyzewski, coach of the Duke Blue Devils men's basketball team, just won his fifth NCAA championship, putting him second on the all-time list behind John Wooden. "Coach K," as he's known, makes no secret that a big part of his success on the court comes from the values he instills in his teams—values that he insists on maintaining. Earlier this season, long before Duke looked like a national contender, he dismissed a key member of his team for failing to live up to the standards he expects everyone on his team to uphold, himself included.

One of Coach K's central values is respect. "Respect is huge," he said. "It's right there with trust, with loyalty, with collective responsibility and pride; being part of something bigger than you."

If you want to be a sticky leader, you also need to be a coach. And if you want to succeed as a coach, you could do worse than meditate on the words of Coach K. He knows a thing or two about winning.

WIN a GAME WORTH PLAYING

When things stall, you have to get them moving again. That's the only way you can achieve the breakthrough you need on the Uphill journey. And to get things moving again, you need a reliable leadership process capable of shifting the status quo.

Sticky leaders call this breakthrough "rules of engagement" and use the acronym OADDA to describe a five-step process that always creates a breakthrough in the status quo. OADDA is simple to learn and becomes more effective with practice. Sticky leaders engaged in a Game worth Playing need to learn it and practice it.

The Coaching Wheel of Leadership Influence

Because leadership is about influence, the OADDA model is called "the coaching wheel of leadership influence." The five elements of OADDA are:

O – Observation
A – Anchoring
D – Define
D – Decide
A – Act

Consider these five elements as presented in a more visual form, in the following pie graphic:

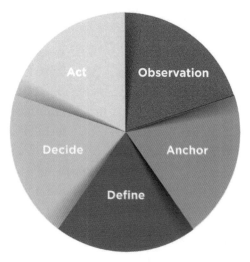

Observation: The first step in the process is to make an observation to identify in detail what is actually occurring. This includes looking for what you want to happen and searching to find evidence of what in fact is happening. Consider the kind of situations where observation becomes very helpful. When you start seeing the following symptoms, you know that you need to find out what's really happening:

- People don't know what to do next.
- People are afraid of something or someone.
- People feel confused.
- You note a lack of belief in self or others: "We can't do this!"
- You sense a lack of clarity.
- People lack the courage to make big requests or ask for what they truly need.
- People feel overwhelmed by too much data; they feel as if they have too much to do, or the task looks too big for the team.

The key to success in the observation phase is to look with "clean eyes" for what is actually taking place, without interpretation or judgment. Seek the facts, observe behaviors, capture what is being said, and look for what isn't being said. Concentrate on a few key questions:

- How do you interpret what you see people doing? Do you see any signs of fear or confusion?
- What are people doing that is working? It always helps to lead with what's already working.
- What are people saying? Pay particular attention to the words used, because they provide important clues to underlying causes.
- How does the atmosphere feel to you? Does it seem "safe"? Are people listening to each other?

Anchoring: Just as a boat uses an anchor to secure its position, so you need to find a few important reference points to make sense of your situation. A few examples of key reference points might include your group's vision, values, goals, previous agreements, rules, and legal requirements. By anchoring your observations to key reference points, you create a clear perspective and build a stable platform for the steps that follow.

Use anchoring to build strength for sustainability as you lead in the Uphill journey toward accomplishing the breakthrough you seek. Ideally, anchoring should help build team confidence and belief that the people involved really can create the breakthrough. If you have doubts about a person on the team, examine your observations and make this one of the first action items you use to build strength in the person you are coaching. Consider some examples of anchoring:

- Anchor on the vision and key commitment areas appropriate to the breakthrough. Get specific about the vision elements and key commitments necessary to persevere.

- Anchor on the corporate values appropriate to the breakthrough or circumstances. Identify them and be ready to reference them.

- Anchor on any previous agreements related to pressing through whatever has you stuck or stalled. Be specific about the goals previously agreed upon. Of utmost importance are the agreements made between you and/or members of the team directly involved in the situation. If you can't identify goals and agreements you have previously agreed upon, you will need to put new ones in place.

- Anchor on your own personal commitment as a leader to model the behavior of perseverance and commitment needed to create the breakthrough. Identify what you will say and do to help others through this difficult time.

- Anchor on the behavior, attitude, past performance and other observations you have made about the people involved, so that you can clearly send the message that they have the ability to accomplish whatever needs to happen. This links directly to what is working, what has worked, and why you believe the breakthrough is possible. Part of the coach's job is to activate hope and confidence.

Define: The coaching conversation really begins once the observation and anchoring phases conclude. The first two steps prepare for the define phase; you share them with the person you are coaching to set the stage for defining why this information is relevant to the circumstances.

Launch the define phase by asking a question designed to reveal what's missing or needs attention, so you can continue your progress toward accomplishing the breakthrough. What anchoring points help you to build the strength required to break through your obstacles? Before you ask your opening questions, reveal the key anchoring points you already have identified. Start with the person and what you appreciate about him or her. Pay close attention to what is working and build safety so you can have an honest conversation.

First, describe what you are observing that is working, to provide hope and assurance that you will all succeed.

Second, ask questions to understand how the person is feeling, linking to what you have observed already. Consider a few examples of how you might do this:

> John, I want you to know I appreciate how you have been coming in early and leaving late as you work on this project. I and everyone else can see your commitment to this breakthrough.

> Andrew, your work on refining our breakthrough plan has brought clarity and agreement to this process.

> Susan, I have noticed how thoughtful you have been in asking questions of others and in sharing your own thinking about the challenges we face in this breakthrough. I appreciate this very much.

Third, present the problem that needs to be resolved and guide the conversation in a way that uses discovery and open dialogue to identify all the elements necessary for a possible solution.

Decide: Once all the information is on the table and everyone has had the opportunity to contribute and be heard, a decision must be made about a course of action. How this decision gets made falls into four different categories: Consult, Vote, Consensus and Command.

- In a consultative form of decision-making, you ask the other party to advise you of a solution. The value of this approach is that it provides a means for ownership and delegation of responsibility to lead the process forward.

- When multiple people are involved, voting on the best course of action can allow the majority to choose how to best proceed.
- In consensus decision-making, the conversation continues until everyone agrees on the solution and process to be used to move forward.
- The command form of decision-making allows you to make the decision for going forward, after hearing the opinions of others. If everyone had their say and a rich dialogue occurred in the Define stage, then others are more likely to positively receive a command decision than if you had just made a decision in a vacuum, on your own.

Transition into the Decide phase by saying something like, "Now, let's review what we have learned through this dialogue." In this process, you review the points of agreement anchored around the purpose of the conversation. Review your notes or what you learned in the Define phase, and lay out the relevant points to be used in deciding, and then make the decision using whatever decision model you have selected.

Act: Nothing happens in leadership without action. This phase involves making the necessary agreement(s), recording them, and making arrangements to follow up and communicate as necessary to ensure things go as planned.

A Way through Difficulty

In every game, players need to follow some winning strategy in order to successfully play the game. For your breakthrough, you need the same kind of effective strategy of play. Once you identify your Game worth Playing, you must develop a strategy that will define the rules of engagement.

Think of a winning strategy as a "way through difficulty." When you uncover the obstacles or constraints as you learn to Love Uphill, you should then aim your game strategy at how to make progress by eliminating or going around the obstacles you've identified.

What kind of leadership energy do you need to design a good strategy? It starts with problem solving (wisdom), but involves all four values in a coordinated fashion.

The process generally begins with the value of power and the energy aimed at results. You ask the question, "What do we need to accomplish here?"

Then the value of love asks its own question: "Who is involved, what do they want, and who can help them get it?" They also ask a vision question: "What does winning look like (success)?" This creates the ideal that everyone can focus on: What do we want to accomplish and who is involved to accomplish it? Getting everyone in agreement by sharing a common vision for success is both powerful and motivating.

Next, the wisdom value comes into play, starting with where we are today and what needs to be done repeatedly to get to where we all can win. The problem solving energy by those who value wisdom crafts a strategy and a process to close the gap between current reality and the ideal defined by the vision of winning.

Finally, we tap those who value knowledge to identify the way everyone can keep score, ensure the rules of engagement are followed, and give everyone a way to "see" how they are playing. They supply the necessary information and make its users accountable for its use.

COACHING CORNER

What do you do when you can see what needs to be done, are leading others as best you can, and still don't see the results you want?

We All Need Grace

Nobody wins every game they play. But there is always another game, another season, and the opportunity to play again. And in every game we play, regardless of the outcome, we need both grace and celebration.

The sticky leader has an important role to play in maintaining the right team attitude and providing encouragement and sustained engagement in the Uphill journey. The first of these two key concepts ought to be familiar to every leader—and sticky leaders know both of them well. Grace allows sticky leaders to maintain momentum and sustain energy moving toward the goal of winning.

One can define grace as both a smooth and attractive way of moving (not stiff or awkward), and as a disposition to act with kindness, courtesy or clemency. Sticky leaders know how to employ grace, even when emotions run high and expectations get missed. This separates them from other types of leaders.

Part of the ability to employ grace in the Uphill journey comes from a deep awareness that winning is an Uphill process and not an event. Keeping people honestly engaged in the Game worth Playing isn't always easy, but it happens more often in the presence of grace, particularly when situations grow difficult.

I've experienced the downside when leaders don't apply grace, and I've also been the beneficiary of grace from leaders who could have painted me as a bad example in front of others.

As a leader, I have failed to apply grace and have seen first-hand the consequences such a failure generates. I've already explained how my company in Guam provided payroll services for many businesses on the island. We had to work hard at avoiding mistakes, because such errors damaged our reputation and cost us financially. Whenever tax changes occurred or when we had to make other programming adjustments, we had to exercise extra care to ensure that we had done our work accurately.

As a programmer myself, I had suffered my share of frustration in trying to get my programs to work correctly. In our growing business, we frequently had to augment our programming capabilities; but because we had little local talent on Guam, we often hired spouses of military personnel who just happened to have the time to work for us. At one point when we needed to make a significant programming change, I assigned that work to a woman who had recently arrived on Guam with her husband, who was stationed at the Naval Air Station. I tasked her to make the required changes prior to running a number of payrolls for our clients. I instructed her in the correct procedures for testing and validating the work and went out of my way to stress the importance of getting things right.

But I never bothered to check her work.

She made the changes, we ran the payrolls, and then distributed them to our clients. Within hours, our phones began to ring, as our clients found multiple errors. I soon discovered we had a huge problem on our hands. I became very upset and angrily confronted my employee. I sternly told her she had to make the corrections herself and then run the payrolls again that evening. I demanded that she fix the huge problem she had created. I went home, feeling good about myself, having shown her who was boss. In my twenty-five-year-old hubris, I patted myself on the back for having demonstrated my authority in such a dramatic way.

On Saturday morning, I came into the office, prepared to inspect the work she had finished overnight. I didn't expect to see her, but there she sat, alone in a dark office—sobbing. She had made her changes, pulled the backup to rerun the payrolls, and then accidently destroyed all the files. Not only had she ruined her work, but we no longer had the files necessary to process the payrolls. We had gone from a single problem to a major disaster.

I'm sure all the color ran out of my face. My self-righteous anger and lack of grace had conspired to kick me over a cliff. And I realized I had no one to blame but myself.

We recovered, but that recovery meant I had to go to each of our clients, collect their prior period reports, and do an extensive bit of work to rebuild files and rerun payrolls. Some of our clients could not pay their employees on time and they had to lean on the grace of their people. Our survival as a company required the grace of our customers! I will never forget that painful, powerful lesson.

Sooner or later, every one of us as leaders needs grace. Therefore we should look for every opportunity to give grace to others. I've learned over many years that people really want to do a good job. When they fail, they generally are harder on themselves than we could ever be on them. Demonstrating grace in the face of difficulty is a hallmark of every sticky leader.

Time to Celebrate

When we succeed as a team, why do we so seldom take time to truly celebrate? Do we fail to see our opportunities to do so, or do we just get too busy to pause to recognize the accomplishments of our coworkers, associates, and other team members?

When did you last pause to celebrate the completion of a season of play? In the Game worth Playing mindset, pausing to celebrate what you've accomplished gives everyone an opportunity to reflect on the effort just expended and to acknowledge each other for their important contributions.

Celebration and gratitude are closely related. Being grateful for the opportunity even to have a Game worth

Playing should trump the actual results we produce. If you hit all your goals, terrific. If you don't, then you can recognize the good effort put forth anyway, and then examine what did work and what you did accomplish, despite having missed the mark.

The best sticky leaders are lifelong learners who recognize that the act of celebration helps fuel the learning process. Celebration provides a way to acknowledge forward movement and growth, regardless of the final results.

The motivational speaker, Zig Ziglar, used to say, "Your altitude will be determined by your attitude." I've found this to be true.

For the last number of years, I have been assembling groups of CEOs to work together in developing their leadership skills. We also work on bringing breakthroughs to their companies, as a matter of practice. Over the course of twelve months, they identify, report on and invest time and effort into (what you now know as) the practice of Sticky Leadership. By the end of the program, some have accomplished their breakthroughs, others have gone way beyond what they initially envisioned, and yet others haven't come close to their breakthrough goals, despite a lot of hard, Uphill work.

Regardless of how everyone ends up, we always complete the program with a celebration of accomplishment. Regardless of the final results, everyone finds something to celebrate and report on to the others. We make a distinction between being "finished" and "complete." Everyone is complete, as the season of the program has ended (the period of play); but some aren't finished and will re-launch a revised breakthrough after the program ends. By sharing both successes and failures, and by highlighting the fun, everyone can celebrate the outcomes they achieved with a group of cohorts they have come to know well.

We measure success in many ways, and regardless of the final score, profits, or losses, it is both valuable and important to celebrate whatever you've completed. Everyone always finds insights and values in the activity of celebrating. We all need to find significant ways of showing our appreciation for one another on our journey together.

It Includes How You Play the Game

No doubt you've heard the old saw that it's not whether you win or lose, but how you play the game. No entrepreneur I know likes or believes in this saying. They all know it really is about winning.

Sadly, however, winning is not always possible. And yet, learning and achieving is. I like the message I recently heard about on a flyer for some new martial arts program: "Here, there are no losers. You either win or you learn."

Sticky Leaders enjoy the game itself, and because of the high purpose of their quest and the inspiring nature of their vision, combined with day-to-day rewards, they keep going. What makes the game fun is the chance to win by targeting breakthroughs to make something good happen.

Leadership is about results, but we don't always get the results we planned. Therefore we remain agnostic about the kind of feedback we get. We know there is no such thing as good news or bad news; there is only news. We can always learn something to improve our play. Loving Uphill keeps us going in our pursuit of winning, and Leading from the Inside Out creates a personal and group development engine that never stops.

If we look at winning as learning, then we *always* win, because we always have something new to learn. Leaders are learners, and when we are learning, we are winning. Those new lessons help us to get better and better.

Winners don't stop. They just keep going, because they have learned to Love Uphill.

EPILOGUE

As I put the final touches on this book, I can't help but think of my friend and first consulting client, Doug Crane. Who knows? Without his encouragement and friendship, I might never have persevered in my own Uphill journey of coaching, training, and consulting with leaders.

When I first began assembling the fundamentals of Vision to Action Leadership (which provides the foundation pieces of Sticky Leadership), he believed in me and encouraged me. Right from the beginning, more than twenty-five years ago, he applied the initial forms of these ideas and practices in his own business, and then hired me as a consultant.

I first met Doug back when I was running marketing for a software company. He responded to an RFP I had crafted for a rather small but challenging project. I was way over my head with ideas I wanted to make happen, and he worked hard to fit within my small budget. That first project led to many more, and we soon became friends. The mutual trust we built made it possible for me to share with him my ideas about building a consulting practice aimed at leadership development for entrepreneurs.

Doug modeled Sticky Leadership in everything he did. We worked closely together for the first few years of my consulting practice, and right from the start, he trusted me to a fault and unflinchingly and boldly applied what became these sticky leadership principles. He taught me that a worthy idea, steadfastly and confidently applied over time, really does work.

Years later, Doug sold his business for millions and rolled some of his money into a family foundation that today funds a unique effort to make the world a better place. The people he employed in his business still count him as a dear friend, and I'm sure they would call working alongside Doug a powerful, life-enhancing experience. Doug knew how to create a Game worth Playing!

Doug's impact on me lasts to this day. Some of the things I learned from him, I still share with others; and I believe they, in turn, pass them along to their own associates. The cool thing about sticky leaders is that what they do goes viral. It propagates in and through others.

In Learning to Love Uphill, Leading from the Inside Out, and creating a Game worth Playing, leaders have just one overarching goal: To develop and maintain attitudes that give them the ability to habitually create breakthroughs.

Our world needs Sticky Leaders! We need *you*. What you know is valuable, what you aspire to is important, and what you are working on now will benefit yourself and others. If your breakthrough is worth doing and you are investing your life energy into it, then it's worth doing well. And achieving it with others has a lasting impact beyond what you may ever know.